# JONATHAN HILL

# THE ILLEGAL ARCHITECT

THE ILLEGAL ARCHITECT FOLLOWS
TWO SIMULTANEOUS JOURNEYS:
ONE CONCEPTUAL, FROM THE
PROFESSIONAL ARCHITECT TO THE
ILLEGAL ARCHITECT, THE OTHER
PHYSICAL, FROM THE ROYAL
INSTITUTE OF BRITISH ARCHITECTS
TO THE PROPOSED INSTITUTE
OF ILLEGAL ARCHITECTS SITED
DIRECTLY IN FRONT OF IT.[1]
THE ENTWINED JOURNEYS ARE

DOCUMENTED IN WORDS AND IMAGES,
EACH PAGE OF TEXT FACING A PAGE
OF DRAWINGS OR PHOTOGRAPHS.
THE INTENTION IS TO EMPHASISE
THE DIFFERENCES BETWEEN THE
WORD AND THE IMAGE AS MUCH
AS THEIR SIMILARITIES, SO AS
TO CREATE AN EXPANSIVE AND
DISCURSIVE PROJECT WITH TWO
DISTINCT BUT RELATED FORMS.

# THE ILLEGAL ARCHITECT

The headquarters of the Royal Institute of British Architects, a building 'commissioned by architects for architects', is located in central London on the corner of Portland Place, a wide road running from north to south, and Weymouth Street, which runs east to west.[2] A row of five sculptures completes the side elevation on Weymouth Street. The central figure of the architect, in the image of Sir Christopher Wren, is flanked by the figures of the painter and sculptor. At the outer edges of the composition are the artisan and mechanic. The sculptures are not separate elements placed on to the facade. They bulge outwards, made physically of the same stone as the building and metaphorically of the same material as the profession. However, the four lesser figures can be understood as either the servants, or the constituent parts, of the architect. The artisan and mechanic are more likely the former and the painter and sculptor the latter, because the manual skills of the artisan and mechanic are judged to be incompatible with the status of the architect, which is dependent upon the contradictory claims to 'autonomy' of professionalism and art.[3]

The concept of the architect (as we now understand the term to mean a designer of architecture and an intermediary in a supervisory capacity between the client and builder) is approximately five hundred years old. During this brief history a number of mutually beneficial relationships have formed between the architect and the state, one of the most cohesive being the Académie Royale d'Architecture, founded in France in 1671, in which the architect performed the role of iconographer of the architecture of the state. The contemporary manifestation of the relationship between the architect and the state is the profession, which began to acquire prominence in the nineteenth century. To the apparent benefit of architects, consumers and the state, the professions fulfilled a need to contain and manage the fluctuations of a rampant industrialised economy which was perceived to be veering close to catastrophe.

All workers defend their activity from outside competition, whether or not they are classified as a profession, but only certain ones are protected by the law. Why can anyone call themselves an artist or a scientist, but not an architect or a doctor? Probably because the latter are in regular direct contact with a public that has little need to deal directly with a scientist or an artist. The role of the professional is primarily to protect rather than to create.

**FIGURE I Components, Institute of Illegal Architects**

The social contract between the state and the profession, by which the title architect is a legal term, offers a (potential) monopoly to the profession in return for the safe management of an area of (unsafe) knowledge.[4]

The theory of autonomous art was defined in the eighteenth century to affirm the economic and political dominance of bourgeois society.[5] As an unquantifiable activity without obvious use, art was isolated from other activities because it was perceived to be incompatible with the rational maximisation of profit required by capitalist society. However, paradoxically, the value of art to capitalist society depended on its exclusion from praxis. It satisfied needs which were suppressed by the demands of production and permitted intellectual speculation which could be exploited for profit, firstly within the art discipline, and then in the industries of mass-production and mass-consumption.[6] At times, architecture has been described as an autonomous, self-referential practice.[7] The recurring claim in architectural historiography, that everything 'outside' the discipline should be expelled in favour of strict, formal analysis, stems from the same ideology as that of the autonomy of art even if it is difficult to squeeze architecture, a diverse and fragmented practice, into art alone.

The model of the architect as professional is reinforced by the law of the state and that of the architect as artist is affirmed by the theory of autonomous art. At first glance, these two strategies appear to be diametrically opposed, but they are similar in that they affirm the fragmentation of society evident in capitalist ideology.

> The dominant tendency fragments space and cuts it up into pieces. Specialisations divide space among them and act upon its truncated parts, setting up mental barriers and practico-social frontiers. Thus architects are assigned architectural space as their (private) property, economists come into possession of economic space, geographers get their own 'place in the sun', and so on.[8]

Each 'specialisation' monitors its space from within. In THEORY OF THE AVANT-GARDE, Peter Bürger distinguishes between the art institution, namely the gallery, and the institution of art, which includes all the codes, phenomena, buildings and objects that constitute the discipline.[9] Although they are sometimes assumed to be the same, the former is just a fragment of the latter. In 1917, Marcel Duchamp exhibited a urinal which he signed 'R. Mutt' and renamed FOUNTAIN. The signature of the artist defines FOUNTAIN as a work of art as much the site of the work.[10] A location in a gallery is but one method by which an object is accorded the status of art which can be acquired by affiliation to the social codes and financial structures of the institution of art wherever the artwork is located.

In architecture there is also a distinction between the architectural institution, primarily represented by the profession, and the institution of architecture, which encompasses all the discipline.[11] However, the internal relations within the disciplines of art and architecture are quite different.[12] In art the two types of institution receive criticism from inside and outside the discipline. The (mythical) autonomy of art is often perceived as a means of marginalising and exploiting art, and whether successful or not, the repeated attacks upon it have had a twofold agenda, first, to diminish the authority of art, the artist and the gallery and, second, to transfer some of that authority to the viewer.[13] The distinction between the artist and the art institution permits the former a degree of critical distance from the latter. It is, however, easier for the artist to avoid the art institution than the institution of art. In architecture, or at least that part of architecture recognised by the profession, criticism tends to come

**FIGURE 2** Component Detail, Institute of Illegal Architects

**FIGURE 3** Component Detail, Institute of Illegal Architects

from outside more often than inside, because the profession binds architects together in a manner unlikely in the art world. The distance between the architect and the architectural institution is virtually non-existent. In art the differences between the artist, art institution and institution of art are recognised. A profession, which is intrinsically conservative and self-protective, must deny such differences, for example those between the architect, the architectural institution and the institution of architecture, because they undermine its claim to securely manage 'unsafe knowledge'.

The profession is the principal architectural institution. Its role is equivalent to that of a police force empowered by the law to monitor architects and architecture. Consequently, the practices and procedures of the architect are the essential tools for the policing of architecture. The architectural profession in Britain is dominated by two bodies, the ARB and RIBA.

The former, the Architects' Registration Board, derives its power directly from the state. It is the legally constituted body appointed to administer and monitor individuals permitted to use the title of architect in the United Kingdom. In line with state and public demands for greater accountability of the professions, its supervisory panel now includes a majority of lay members. The ARB has the power to discipline and remove a member from the list of architects. Architects must be registered with the ARB, but need not be a member of the RIBA, although a majority choose to be. The Royal Institute of British Architects is the principal mechanism for the protection and propagation of the cultural and social status of the profession. The RIBA and ARB are housed on adjacent sites in the centre of London, rather like the conflicting halves of a pantomime donkey. The RIBA, the public face of the profession, is located in a grand and elegant building on the route between Regent's Park and Regent Street. The ARB is sited in a nondescript building in a side street at the rear of the RIBA.

**FIGURE 4 Exterior, Institute of Illegal Architects.** The Institute of Illegal Architects inhabits the public domain of the street rather than the private realm of the familiar building site. It is sited in Portland Place directly in front of the RIBA. The IIA consists of five spaces and a series of transient elements. Each space is conceived for a specific form of sensual or perceptual production—sound, smell, touch, sight and time—but a tight fit between space and occupation is not expected and is even undesirable. The five spatial zones are hinged around the horizontal plane of the street, so that they appear to be rising from, and sinking into, Portland Place. Flush with the surface of the street, the Production Space for Time occupies the full width of Portland Place for 250 metres between Devonshire Street and Cavendish Street, blocking the street to vehicular traffic and severing the symbolic route from Regent's Park to Regent Street, a sequence of spaces that forms one of the few architectural manifestations of royal patronage in London.[14] The centre line of the Production Space for Time, where the surface changes from white to black, is aligned with the Weymouth Street elevation of the RIBA. The Production Space for Sound, a flattened cone sited directly in front of the RIBA, is balanced on the Production Space for Smell, a concave glass shell recessed into the Production Space for Time. The Production Space for Touch is located under the Production Space for Time. The linear Production Space for Sight and an underground ramp protrude into the section of Weymouth Street to the west of Portland Place. The Production Space for Sight cantilevers over the Production Space for Sound, to focus on the eye level of an individual leaving the entrance of the RIBA.

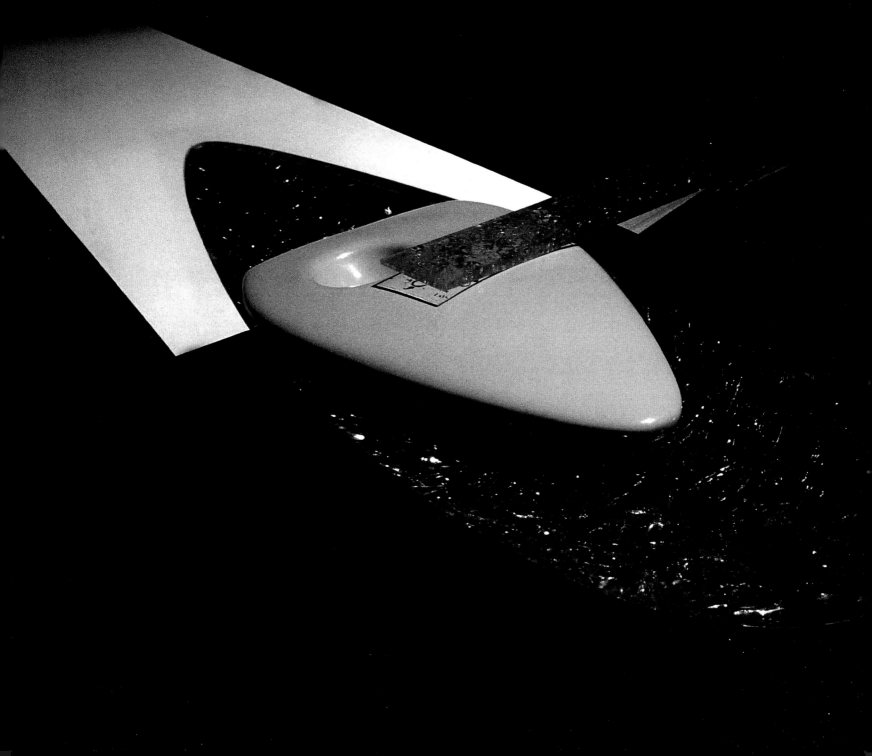

Home is the one place, the one architecture, that is perceived to be truly personal. Home always belongs to someone. It is supposedly a stable vessel for the personal identity of its occupant(s), a container for, and mirror of, the self. But the concept of home is also a response to insecurity and the fear of change. A home must appear stable because social norms and personal identity are actually shifting and slippery. Home is a metaphor for a threatened society and the threatened individual. It is an intense manifestation of interiority aligned against exteriority. The safety of the home is really the sign of its opposite, a certain nervousness, a fear of the tangible or intangible dangers inside and outside.[15]

Directly opposite the RIBA, on the other side of Portland Place, is the most prominent building of the embassy of the People's Republic of China. The flag hanging on the facade clearly states the building's purpose and importance. An embassy performs a number of roles—it is both a home(land) for its citizens and a police station to protect and discipline insiders and monitor and exclude outsiders.

In pre-Communist China the height of a dwarf wall at the threshold of a house represented the social status of the occupant, permitting an immediate comparison between visitor and visited. In Communist China, the size of an apartment precisely indicated the status of its occupant(s).[16] Social status can be made manifest in architecture if it is desirable for it to be seen and understood. In THE WAY OF MASKS, Claude Lévi-Strauss suggests that a mask transforms and omits more than it represents.[17] Therefore, in the study of masks, it is essential to discover what is denied even more than what is revealed. The mask and the building are similar apparatuses through which ideology is transmitted, transformed and concealed. Individuals and groups can be excluded from the dominant power structures by the process of mythification evident in a building, which makes a situation, or system, appear impenetrable and defines the identity of the 'outsider'.

A foreigner requires a visa to enter China. The visa section of the embassy is located down the street from the main building on the ground floor of a house that gives virtually no indication of its role. The visitor to the embassy is analogous to the foreigner in China: aware of the scale of the whole, but permitted to enter just a part. An individual is defined as an outsider very directly, being permitted to use the side door rather than

FIGURE 5 Institute of Illegal Architects as Viewed From the RIBA. The Institute of Illegal Architects is neither Royal, nor British. It fosters what the profession omits: the production of architecture by the illegal architect and the active user. The relationship between the RIBA and the IIA is similar to that between the body and the fair-ground mirror that fattens, slims or distorts the 'original', inviting both laughter and nightmares.

the front one. If the main embassy building is the mask, the control of the population within China, whether native or foreign, is the omission.

Allegiance is defined as loyal support to one's nation, cause or ideology. Allegiance to a profession is not dissimilar to allegiance to a nation and just as blind.[18] The buildings of the RIBA and ARB are the embassy of the architectural profession, combining the roles of home and police station. The physical restrictions on the visitor to the RIBA are less direct than those on the foreigner entering the Chinese embassy. The non-architect enters through the main entrance of the RIBA and is encouraged to use the book shop, exhibitions and café. So what is omitted from this mask? What threat is posed to this home? The answer to both questions is any individual outside the architectural profession who produces architecture. The non-architect is permitted to enter the RIBA as a consumer but not as a producer of architecture. The RIBA is equivalent to the main building of the Chinese embassy but, while the latter clearly excludes foreigners, the former presents the illusion of accessibility. As there are no short-term visas into the architectural profession, it has no space equivalent to the visa section of the Chinese embassy. Consequently, the ARB is not the visa section but the passport office, placed firmly out of sight.

The primary role of the RIBA and ARB is to protect the profession. As defined by Pierre Bourdieu, the accumulation of cultural capital has a direct bearing on financial and social status and is affected by gender, occupation, class and race, which can help or hinder its acquisition.[19] An architect acquires cultural capital as an individual and collectively as a member of a profession. Through the contract between state and profession, the architect seeks to acquire cultural capital, the value of which, however, is not assured and has to be defended.[20] While the legal status of the architect is administered through the ARB, the aim of the RIBA is to protect and extend the cultural capital of individual architects and the profession, one adding to the other.

The architectural profession claims a monopoly over a specific area of architectural production for the purpose of economic and social self-protection. The principal aim of the profession is to provide the products and practices of its members with an iconic status and a cultural value, to suggest that only the work of architects deserves the title architecture. Architects monitor and patrol their domain in order to exclude critics from within and intruders from without. They deride any threat as ignorant or mistaken and imply that there is a truthful and correct interpretation of a fixed body of knowledge. Shortly after the 1997 general election, a survey in the RIBA JOURNAL, the magazine of the profession, asked the victorious Labour Party's new Members of Parliament: "Do great buildings need architects?". To this 96% answered yes. In an arrogant summary the RIBA JOURNAL added: "Luckily, Labour's new MPs, however ignorant of the process of architecture, understand overwhelmingly that great buildings are only possible through architecture.".[21] The most revealing aspect of this statement occurs at the end of the sentence, where architecture is used in place of architects. The assumption that they are the same is the guiding principle of the profession.[22]

The knowledge that architecture is, however, not just the work of architects, increases the desire of the profession to claim architecture as its 'private property'.[23] Consequently, architects attempt to prevent two intrusions, one into the body of their profession, the other into the body of their architecture. The former occurs when the work of an illegal architect is recognised as architecture. The latter occurs when the user occupies

**FIGURE 6 Frontal Axonometric, Tomb of the Architect, Production Space for Time, Institute of Illegal Architects.** The Tomb of the Architect is recessed into the southern section of the Production Space for Time. Set into the ground are four reinforced concrete tombs with padded rubber interiors. Flush with the ground, a toughened glass skin seals each tomb. The tombs contain thirty elements from the office and home. All the elements are alive except Number 18 (the architect). Previously assumed to be dead, the architect (white, male and heterosexual) now trusts in re-incarnation. A periscope at the end of the supply duct casts a cloud of ashes and black ink every time the architect appears to move.

architecture. To repel these intrusions, architects assume that architecture is a physical phenomenon with specific materials and dimensions, a building but not any building, their building (preferably) unoccupied. In architectural practice and discourse, the experience of architecture is the experience of the architect, who lays claim to both the production and reception of architecture.

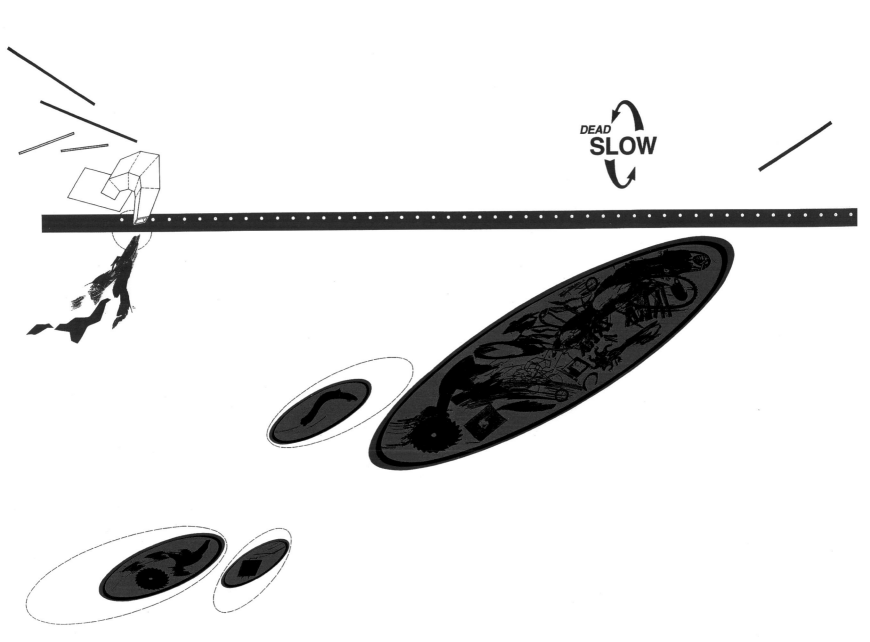

To affirm its claim to be the sole producer of architecture, the profession initiates a number of protectionist measures. The ideological relations of a discipline are rarely criticised from within. Cultural practices police their boundaries by suppressing internal discussions that undermine their integrity or question their role, status and function in society. In any historical period, architectural practice adopts a number of forms and roles, but usually one purpose, code and set of restrictions dominates the others. The limits of architecture, as understood by architects, are defined through the means of visual and verbal languages which appear to be ever-present and self-justifying. Architects attempt a sleight of hand in which a building is displaced by a photograph (of an empty building), a drawing (of an unbuilt project) or a theory (of an abstracted architecture). They then proceed to discuss the photograph, drawing or theory as if it were the building. As the former are far easier to control than the latter the architectural profession can, in an act of self-delusion, sustain its 'mastery' of architecture.

The principal weapon against the illegal architect is the legal status of the architect. The user is harder to ignore and therefore the tactics deployed are more complicated. Western discourse is founded on a series of dualisms, each with a 'superior' and 'inferior' component. The two terms in a dualism are dependent upon each other, their relationship is far more subtle than one of mere opposition. One term seeks to define itself in relation to the other, to suggest a degree of separateness which may be illusory. In architecture the architect is assumed to be the superior term and the user the inferior one. Architects have two strategies to maintain this hierarchy. The first is to assume that a building need not be occupied for it to be recognised as architecture, the second is to attribute to the user forms of behaviour acceptable to the architect. The former can be summarised as removing the user, the latter as controlling the user. Both strategies are enforced through the familiar languages of architectural production and discourse.

**FIGURE 7 Frontal Axonometric, Northern Section of the Production Space for Time, Institute of Illegal Architects.** The Production Space for Time is divided into two halves. The northern half is made of a hard black stone covered with a 50 mm layer of soft white chalk, the southern half is made of a hard white stone covered with a 50 mm layer of soft black chalk. Movement across the surface gradually erases the chalk surfaces, so that the northern half changes from black to white, the southern half from white to black. Mixed in with the chalk are the seeds of wild plants with either black or white flowers. The chalk and seeds are dispersed through the city on the shoes of pedestrians. Once all the soft chalk has been removed, the harder surface beneath erodes more slowly. At the northern edge of the space there are seven periscopes that transfer sights, sounds and smells of the IIA into the RIBA and vice versa. The periscopes all look the same.

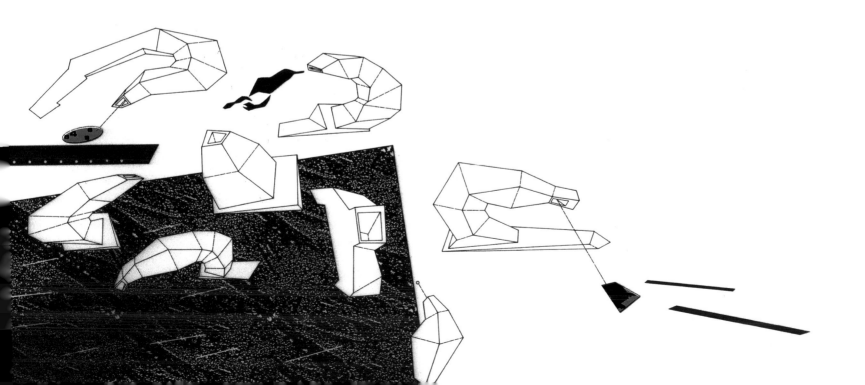

The most blatant denial of the user occurs in the photograph, which empties a building of its inhabitants. The absence of people from the architectural photograph is the physical manifestation of a deep fear of the user within the architectural profession, a condition also evident in the architectural drawing. Architects draw buildings. They do not make them. The drawing is the principal language of mediation between the architect and the builder. Therefore, architects can only control what they can represent in words or images.[24] For architects, the gap between the drawing and the building is an uncomfortable truth to be forcefully denied because it threatens their authority over architecture. All forms of representation omit as much as they include. The architectural perspective usually contains a crowd of people but it is rare to find a photograph of an inhabited building. So where have they all gone? The answer is that they were never really there to begin with. The perspective is usually produced to persuade a client. It is a mask to the design process. The principal drawings used by the architect, such as plans, sections and elevations, have limited means with which to describe or consider the inhabitation of architecture. If the photograph empties architecture after the event, the drawing empties it beforehand.

The drawing, and to a certain degree the photograph, perform a role somewhat similar to the transitional object, a term used in psychoanalysis. For a child this may, for example, be a teddy bear. Its role is positive and 'a defence against separation from the mother', to be discarded when no longer needed. If the child is unable to make this transition, the result can be: "the fixed delusion which may turn the transitional object into that permanent security prop, the fetish, both in the Freudian sense (it disguises the actuality of lack) and in the Marxian sense (it functions as a commodity that supplies human want).".[25] The drawing, and other means by which the architect either denies or claims to control the user, are equivalent to an undiscarded transitional object. Like a child who cannot discard a teddy bear, the architect who fails to look beyond the drawing is unable to reach a level of mature self-awareness.

**FIGURE 8 View Along the Length of the Production Space for Sight Towards the RIBA, Institute of Illegal Architects.** Seventy metres in length, and triangular in plan, section and elevation, the Production Space for Sight forms a distorted perspective. The eye level of an individual leaving the RIBA is aligned with the glazed horizontal edge of the space, which increases in depth but narrows in width as it moves away from the RIBA. The architect, on the steps of the RIBA, looks directly down the full length of the interior and the illegal architects look back. The interior exaggerates and subverts the solitary nature of computing, reading, writing and drawing. It is wide enough for only one row of seating, a seventy-metre long sofa upholstered in lycra. The sofa becomes progressively softer as it moves away from the RIBA. Its sumptuous softness and the absence of armrests invite contact between the occupants. The walls and roof of the building are built of timber. The whole space is then faced in glass, which also forms the floor. A stainless steel grater and a paper shredder, set within the side walls, gradually fill the gap between the timber and glass with grated timber, shredded texts and drawings. At the end furthest from the RIBA, the Production Space for Sight sinks into western section of Weymouth Street and a wide timber ramp leads down into the Production Space for Touch.

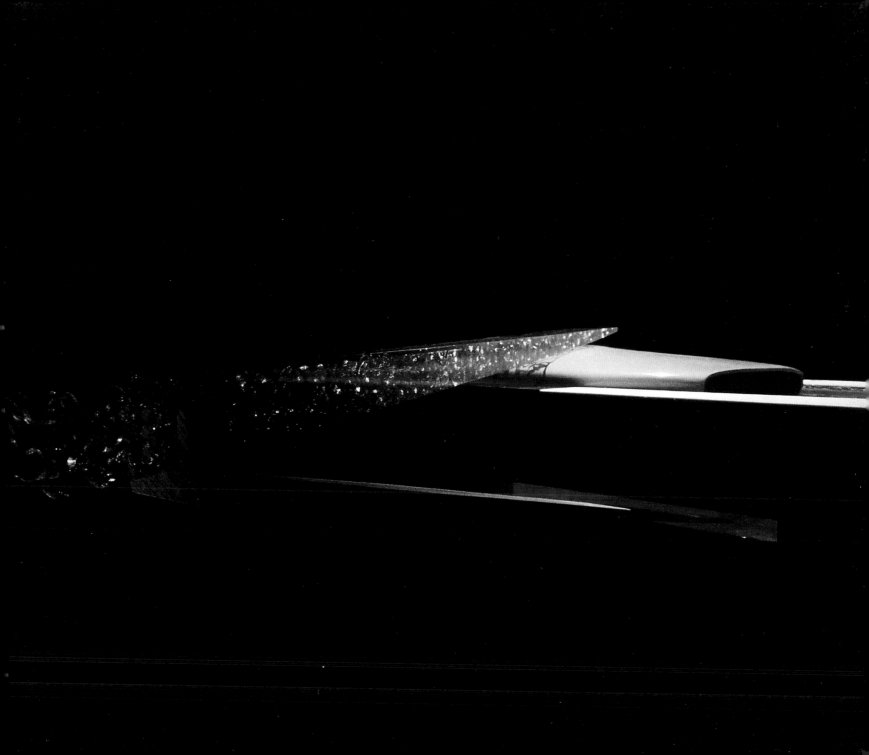

If the photograph and the drawing exclude the user, architectural discourse includes the user under controlled conditions. To consider the inhabitation of architecture, architects appropriate, from other disciplines, forms of experience more manageable and limited than the ones evident in the everyday occupation of architecture. In the first half of this century, the most influential of these was the scientific management of labour.[26] It is easy to understand why determinism is so attractive to architects because it assumes that the actions of the user are predictable.[27] It is the most contradictory and alarming aspect of the Modernist agenda because, from the architect, it demands a faith in science that cannot be validated scientifically and, from the user, it expects merely obedience.

With a few exceptions, early twentieth century Modernism discarded visual references to the human form.[28] Instead, it concentrated on the actions and processes of the body. Functionalism supposes that only the quantifiable is real. It disregards non-productive, 'irrational' actions and focuses only on actions deemed to be 'useful'.[29] In 1927 Grete Schütte-Lihotzky designed the mass-produced, standardised Frankfurt Kitchen for the city's social housing programme. In applying the scientific management of labour to the production of architecture, Schütte-Lihotzky analysed the actions performed within the kitchen in order to eradicate unnecessary labour and enable each function to be carried out with the minimum effort and in the minimum space. Efficiency rather than pleasure was her agenda. The Frankfurt Kitchen is an appropriate emblem for the rational, waste-free society propagated by Functionalists, in which the paradigmatic form of the body is the technician at work in the factory and the home. Le Corbusier's phrase, "a machine for living in", is only an accurate description of Functionalist sensibilities if the human is a component of the machine not the machine a servant of the human.[30] The "machine for living in" is a totalising and all-pervading model for society as well as architecture. The desire for a society of scientific progression and functional purity is similar to the obsessive hand-washing in individuals. They are both a product of social anxiety but on different scales. In Alvar Aalto's Paimio Sanatorium, an iconic Functionalist project, the surfaces of the hand-basins are carefully angled to silence running water as its falls into the basin below, both to deny the presence of dirt and to hide the process of cleansing.[31] The silent flow of dirty water

FIGURE 9 View Along the Production Space for Sight Towards the RIBA, Institute of Illegal Architects.

disappearing into the drains is the sound of guilty minds at work, 'improving' society through architecture.

Two further models are particularly prevalent, the actor on the stage and the viewer in the gallery. Beatriz Colomina discusses the user as an actor in a comparison of the houses of Loos and Le Corbusier.[32] In the former, the occupant of the house is placed at the edges of the interior, looking inwards.[33] In the latter, the occupant is pushed to the edges of the interior, looking outwards.[34] Colomina further relates that the photographs of the respective interiors are normally empty of people but, in the former, a visitor is constantly expected while, in the latter, there are signs of an occupant having recently departed. Colomina proposes a fascinating analogy between the occupant and the actor. In a Loosian house, the occupant is a theatrical actor, in a Corbusian one, a filmic actor. Of course, the analogy of user to actor suits architects because it suggests that the relation of architect to user is that of director to directed.

In an attempt to maintain and reproduce the aura of art, which despite protestations to the contrary still maintains a hold over the familiar perception of art, the art institution requires precise codes of behaviour, particularly silence and reverence.[35] The traditional art object in the gallery demands the physically distanced, passive contemplation of the viewer, for whom meaning is anchored to the artist. Consequently, the reception of art is isolated and internalised, not collective and political. Placed in a hermetic enclosure and protected against decay from heat, light and time, the artwork is seen but rarely touched. No trace or mark is left by the viewer, who is absorbed and distanced at the same time. This is not the familiar experience of architecture but it is regularly defined in terms similar to art, from which it acquires much of its status. Ironically, an architect's experience of architecture is more akin to the contemplation of the art object in a gallery than the occupation of a building.[36] Unfortunately, architects often choose to ignore this simple distinction. For architects, the classification of architecture not just as an art, but as an art similar to painting or sculpture, is a social and financial necessity because the theory of autonomous art is most closely associated with gallery based art. Modelled on art history, histories of architecture discuss the building as an object of artistic contemplation and imply that this is the familiar experience of architecture. The photograph acts as the mediator between the writer and the reader, who is encouraged to equate the experience of a photograph with the experience of a building. Consequently, in architectural discourse, the object of discussion is often the photograph not the building because the former, rather than the latter, most closely fulfils the desires and expectations of the architect and historian for an object of artistic contemplation.

Sometimes the experience of architecture is scientifically predictable. Although not an everyday occurrence, the occupant of architecture is occasionally equivalent to an actor, especially one heavily into improvisation. It is also possible to experience architecture in circumstances similar to the contemplation of art. However, these models have little relevance to an understanding of architecture. They tell us far more about what architects and critics would like to be the experience of architecture. Instead of an intelligent discussion of architectural occupation we find models based on science, theatre and art. It is quite shocking to realise that the experience of architecture receives so little serious discussion within the profession. If the user appears at all it is obliquely in the discussion of other issues, which have themselves, until recently, been marginalised, such as sexuality.[37] It is highly noticeable that although the creativity of the 'reader' is

FIGURE 10 View to the North Towards the Production Spaces for Sight and Sound, Institute of Illegal Architects.

discussed outside the profession, it is largely ignored inside the profession, which still maintains that the user is a stable, centralised and passive subject, if he or she is acknowledged at all.[38]

The adversarial relationships between producer and user evident in architectural practice are countered in a number of cultural disciplines. The re-formulation of subject-object relationships occurs at two levels: a cross-disciplinary one, such as Donna Haraway on technology, and a disciplinary one, such as Roland Barthes on literature and Dan Graham on art.[39]

Land, performance, conceptual and installation art are in part an attempt to deny the commodity status of art. In contrast to the detached contemplation of art described by Bürger as the purpose of art in bourgeois society, they demand a more discursive engagement between the work and its audience. In contemporary art, subject-object relations and the forms of perception are often the central focus of production as well as discourse.[40] The subject is recognised as being an active, engaged participant, not a passive, empty vessel. Installation art is possibly the closest art form to architecture. Although neither a location inside or outside the gallery avoids the defining codes of the institution of art, installation art constantly questions the boundaries of art, demanding a more critical and sensual relationship between object and subject than the primarily visual one of the traditional artwork.[41]

Haraway implies that whether attached to us physically, like the heart pacemaker, or perceptually, like the television, we are machine and human. Once we understand perspective, film or the internet, the machine is in our minds even more than our bodies. We cannot remove it, just as we cannot remove the technology of our human bodies: the heart, lungs, liver and brain. "By the late twentieth century, our time, a mythic time, we are all chimeras, theorised and fabricated hybrids of machine and organism; in short we are cyborgs."[42] Many of the arguments for the superficiality and emptiness of contemporary culture rely on the dominance of technology over humanity, the flattening of thought to the empty abstraction of science.[43] But if we are cyborgs, a hybrid of metal and muscle, the struggles occur within us and through our actions. The machine is no longer negative, certainly no more or no less so than the human. Haraway accepts the existence of the human and the machine, the two terms of a binary coupling, but suggests that they are present in the same person. Her argument refers specifically to technology but offers a subtle revision of all dualisms. Rather than the hierarchical relations of binary oppositions, Haraway proposes a system of mutual dependencies. Applied to architecture, this suggests that the architect and user are not distinct and separate entities, necessarily antagonistic towards each other, but exist within each other: the user being an (illegal) architect.

My understanding of the user of architecture is primarily indebted to Roland Barthes' "The Death of the Author". Barthes does not suggest the death of writing but the death of the particular type of author who proposes a uniform, organic system of meaning based upon mimesis, the belief that an image, word or object is the carrier for a fixed message determined by the author. Barthes states that the importance of the author is over-rated because the journey from author to text to reader is never direct or one-way. The text often contradicts the intentions of the author and the reader always constructs a new text in the act of reading. Barthes' denunciation of the symbolic purity of language recalls, first, Benjamin's support for allegory as a more plastic form of communication than the symbol and, second, Surrealist practices that shift the emphasis from the single author to hybrid author-readers who both make and consume a work.[44] Barthes recognises that a profusion of ambiguities and interpretations inhabit the gap between writing and reading but does not imply that the writer should

**FIGURE II The Eye and the Ear, Institute of Illegal Architects.** The Production Space for Sight cantilevers over the Production Space for Sound. The eye level of an individual walking down the steps at the entrance of the RIBA is aligned with the glazed horizontal edge of the former, which, at one and a half metres above ground level, is the highest point of the Institute of Illegal Architects. The circular recessed 'ear' in the latter projects the sounds of production into the RIBA.

be without ideas. Instead, he proposes that the writer should be aware of, and indeed use, the limitations of a medium. Barthes, therefore, argues for the death of the traditional author and the creation of a new writer, aware of the importance of the reader. Barthes' reformulation of the author suggests a new model for the architect, one who recognises that the inhabitation of architecture is itself a creative activity.[45] In literature there is not a clear linear route from the author to reader, neither is there one in architecture from the architect to the user.

"The Death of the Author" has a considerable, and comparatively unexplored, relevance to architecture. However, a building is not directly comparable to a text. Rather than linking one term within literature to another in architecture, I suggest that author-text-reader relations, as a whole, are analogous to architect-building-user relations.[46] Architecture is the gap between building and using, just as literature is the gap between writing and reading.

If the architect is to learn from the new definitions of subject-object relationships it is important to recognise how the experience of architecture is different to that of literature and art. Determinism assumes that the architectural user is passive and predictable while this text seems to suggest that the user is active and unpredictable. But both are true. The oscillation between passivity and activity is more apparent in the experience of architecture than in most other cultural phenomena.

Hannah Arendt cites the mediocrity of evil, recognising that evil is not necessarily the result of a singular large event but is also found in small events which acquire scale through repetition and the obedience of a specific population.[47] As the entry point of the European colonial powers into China, Shanghai was divided into a series of quarters based on nationality. The waterfront promenade, the Bund, provides a complete panorama of European colonial architecture. During the occupation of Shanghai, a sign in the small park at the end of the Bund stated who was excluded from the gardens: 'No Dogs or Chinese'. The story of this small sign, which encapsulates the racism of western colonialism, is told to Shanghaiese schoolchildren.[48] However, the park is still there but the sign is not. Therefore, there are really two parks with a single form on the same site: the one experienced by the visitors who know nothing of its history and the one used by the Shanghaiese who know about the sign. We never experience the same architecture. Neither do we perceive it purely as an individual because of the range of our cultural and social affiliations.

Although architecture does not just consist of buildings, the experience of a building is a model of the relationships between subject and object in architecture. The park in Shanghai is, therefore, unusual because its reputation may precede experience, a situation more common in other media. Value, authority, and the desired interpretation of a film, book or exhibition is disseminated to its public through hype, reviews and the codes of the space in which it is displayed. The mass media with the largest audiences also have the most extensive means to publicise a particular interpretation. As a text or artwork usually has a much smaller audience than a film, the mechanisms for the dissemination of a 'correct' reading are less pervasive in the former than the latter but they are more intense because the cultural value ascribed to art and literature is higher

FIGURE 12 **Production Space for Sound, Institute of Illegal Architects.** The Production Space for Sound, a flattened steel cone covered internally and externally in rubber, is sited directly in front of the RIBA. The circular recess, or 'ear', in its upper surface is adjacent to the corner of the RIBA at the junction of Portland Place and Weymouth Street.

than that of film and, consequently, greater authority is accorded to the statements of the artist and writer than the film-maker. In contrast, few buildings reach mass consciousness. They are experienced in relation to other buildings known to the user, but without a knowledge of their history or the architect's publicity, of which only other architects are usually aware. A film, artwork or book is experienced at most a few times, but may have a second and equally powerful existence in memory. A building, however, is usually experienced over a long period of time and even the occupant of a large city frequents a narrow range of places and routes. Therefore, while most media are experienced in a state of focused, but often submissive, concentration, architecture is experienced in a state of distraction. The attention of the user is seemingly focused on everything but the building. Even in the case of the park in Shanghai, the focus of the user is on the sign rather than the more obviously architectural elements.

A plethora of cultural and social codes reinforce the superiority of art over the everyday, of contemplation over distraction, of sight over the other senses. It appears that architecture is demeaned by its association with distraction. "Habit is the ballast that chains the dog to his vomit."[49] The contemplation of art reinforces the hierarchy of the senses prevalent within western culture. Contemplation is primarily a form of visual awareness in which sound, smell and touch are, as far as possible, eradicated. If judged on vision alone, the concentrated gaze of the visitor in a gallery is superior to the distracted attention of the occupant of architecture. But, if awareness of all the senses is taken into account, the complexity of architectural occupation can be recognised. Architecture is experienced in a state of distraction but not a state of unawareness.[50] It is a particular type of awareness that enables a person to perform, at the same time, a series of complex activities that move in and out of focus from a conscious to an unconscious level.[51] In architecture, habit and memory are coupled with the sensual disembodiment associated with twentieth century forms of communication to form a complex compound of spatial and temporal layers. Someone talks to you, caresses your back, while you listen to the phone, read the fax and peer out of the window. Architecture is experienced collectively and individually, each facet of a person reacting to a space in distinct and perhaps conflicting ways.

It is clear that architecture, as defined by the architectural profession, is different to architecture as experienced by its users. Within this contradiction are located many of the dilemmas of architectural practice. To acquire financial and social security, a profession needs a defined area of knowledge with precise contents and limits. In "Building an Architect", Mark Cousins distinguishes between strong and weak disciplines.[52] The interior of a strong discipline is precise and visible, its boundaries equally certain; decisions are made only in reference to what is already inside the discipline. A strong discipline contains internal self-validating codes that safely protect its members and exclude 'ignorant' outsiders. Cousins distinguishes a strong discipline, such as one of the natural sciences, which is primarily concerned with objects, from a weak discipline, such as architecture, in which the effect of an object on a subject is of fundamental importance. Architecture is, however, not weak in a pejorative sense but weak in contrast to a self-validating, object-centred discipline. In architecture,

**FIGURE I3 Aerial Perspective Looking North, Production Space for Sound, Institute of Illegal Architects.** The interior surface of the Production Space for Sound progresses from hard at the entrance to soft and upholstered at the rear. A pivoting storage door with four recessed nozzles is set within the south facade, which consists of two parallel sheets of glass with a 150 mm void between them. Pigment, seed and polystyrene from the storage door is blown into, and sucked out, of the void between the sheets of glass, turning the facade from transparent to opaque and back to transparent. The periscopes on the storage door project the sights and smells of production into the RIBA. Other Transient Elements in the drawing: Modulator (02) Eye contact initiates a sensual response from a catalogue of muted sounds, smells, and sights. Suitcase (13) The travelling case houses slide projection equipment, a microphone and speakers. Architect (18) White, male, heterosexual, and previously presumed to be dead, he now trusts in reincarnation. Frame (45) Used for scaling, it contains a glass door that can be looked through but not opened. Television (78) A 1960s appliance produced by Piretta in Italy specifically for indoor and outdoor use. Fan (80) Activated by eye contact, it operates at a number of speeds but is always totally silent.

the boundary between inside and outside is confused and there is no shared idea of what constitutes its interior. Trying to limit architecture is like pouring water into a colander. There are simply too many holes.

The state offers legal protection to a profession in return for the management of a specific area of knowledge. The guardian of a strong discipline, such as the lawyer, is able to fulfil his or her side of the bargain; the architect is not. This is deeply disturbing to the architectural profession, whose social and financial status depends upon its ability to control the practice of architecture. "The urge to make separations, between clean and dirty, ordered and disordered, 'us and them', that is, to expel and abject, is encouraged in western cultures, creating feelings of anxiety because such separations can never be finally achieved."[53]

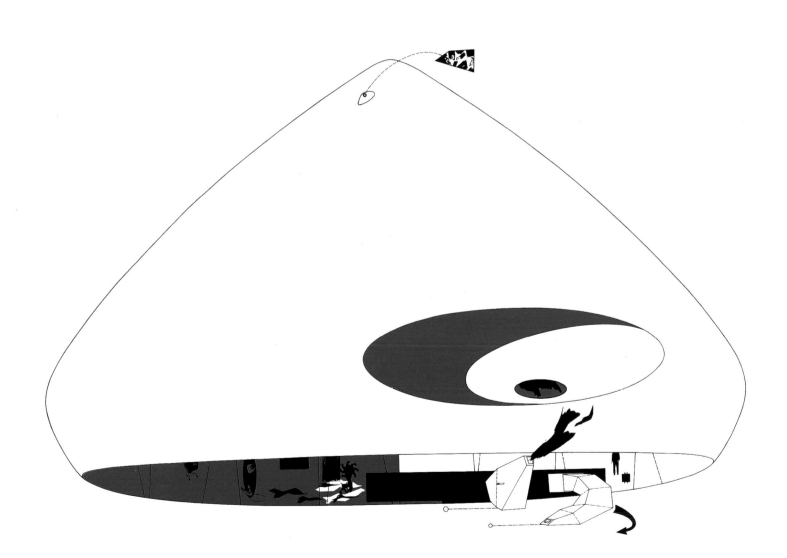

Professionalism and art dominate architectural discourse and practice and architects appear to have very good reasons to support each 'autonomy'. The former because it offers the architect the protection of the law and the status of an 'objective' expert, the latter because it offers architecture the aura of art and the architect the status of the 'subjective' artist. However, as a profession is compatible with a strong discipline but not a weak one based on subject-object relationships, the status of the architect as a professional is at best problematic and at worst contradictory. So what about the other autonomy? How often is the work of an architect recognised as art?

The status of the architect as an artist cannot be assessed on its own as it is affected, and threatened, by the actions of individuals or groups who claim a part of architectural practice. Donald Judd is classified as an artist, but he is also the designer of the buildings of the Chinati Foundation in Marfa, a small Texan town on the border with Mexico. One of the major buildings in the town is the former Marfa National Bank, in which, with enjoyable but presumably unconscious irony, Judd located his 'Architecture Studio'.[54] In claiming the practice of architecture as well as that of art, Judd added to his own cultural capital and financial status. However, producing architecture is different from being an architect. The architect is protected in law, but architecture is not, a situation which implies that a person can make architecture but not be an architect, a category to which Judd would appear to belong. However Judd would have gained comparatively little from the legal acquisition of the title of architect because his work, including his architecture, acquires its most significant cultural capital from art. As the producer of acclaimed art, it is accepted that Judd's architecture is also art.

The financial value of an artwork is related to the cultural capital of its author. Irrespective of actual quality, the art of a famous artist is more valuable than that of a lesser known one but a respected architect is rarely paid more than an ordinary one, implying that the value of architecture as an art is not fully recognised in the hands of an architect.

The status of the architect is uncertain precisely because it is subject to the contradictory demands of art and the profession.[55] Architects are badly paid for their knowledge and skill, suggesting that the status of the architect as both professional and artist is low. Architects gain little from the profession or from art, because in claiming to belong to both they

FIGURE 14  Perspective Looking North, Production Space for Sound, Institute of Illegal Architects. Directed at the RIBA, the triangular Production Space for Sight cantilevers over the Production for Sound. Transient Elements in the drawing: Modulator (02) Eye contact initiates a sensual response from a catalogue of muted sounds, smells, and sights. Suitcase (13) The travelling case houses slide projection equipment, a microphone and speakers. Kitchen (17) An oven and freezer are housed within a corrugated steel casing coupled to a marble fireplace. Cleaner (21) Compensates for signs of order by dirtying the interior with an appropriate sound, sight or smell. Table (43) Formed from four materials: plastic, steel, wood and soap, each exactly the same colour—orange.

belong to neither. In order to gain from art, which is compatible with a weak discipline based on subject-object relationships, the architect must first discard, or at least transform, the profession.

In return for its pact with the state, the architectural profession is required to be the police force of architecture and architects. But the control of architecture by its police force is partial and mythical and a myth sometimes does most harm to the social group it seems to protect. Professionalism acts as a restraint on architects because it encourages them to be parochial and conservative. Ideas and actions that challenge the authority of the architectural profession are marginalised and, consequently, the language of architectural practice acts as a restriction as much as a liberation. So many of the important qualities of architecture appear only fleetingly in the architectural drawing, model and text. Therefore, they are not designed by the architect. It is questionable who is hurt more by this situation, the architect or the user, as both are marginalised.

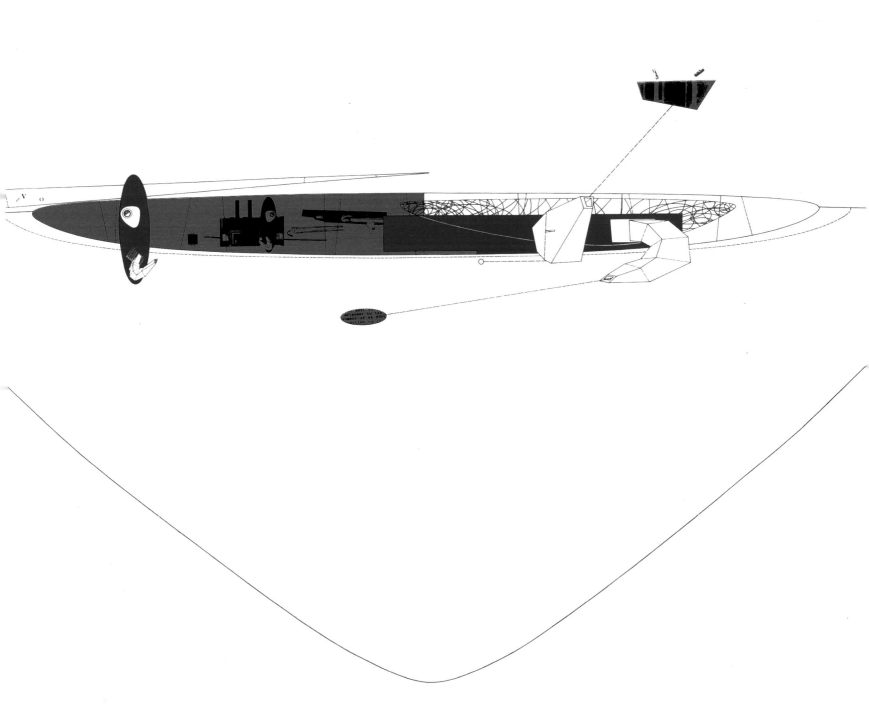

It is difficult to estimate the effects of the loss of legal protection for the architectural profession. The use of one term, architect, to describe all architects masks the diversity of architectural practices and practitioners. Some would gain and others loose from the removal of legal status. Individuals now on the periphery of architectural practice would undoubtedly abuse the term, but separating the architect from the law would allow new types of architect to develop from both inside and outside the profession.

All disciplines resist incursions from 'outside' whilst they also influence, and are affected by, the practices they resist. Sometimes the relationship is less antagonistic. A cross-cultural approach to architecture is now quite common, although this occurs more in words than deeds. Relating one discipline to another is nearly always likely to be productive but architecture needs to be joined to those disciplines which counter the tendencies of architects towards abstraction rather than those that may affirm it. In this regard, geography or anthropology may be more useful than philosophy. Transitions between disciplines can be invaluable, but the act of crossing from one to another is not enough in itself. The reasons for the move need to be stated and understood. Why does a geographer choose to discuss architecture for instance? What is missing in geography and found in architecture? The opposite is equally relevant. Should there be a geographer-architect or a doctor-architect?

The architect is enshrined in law but architecture has no legal protection. Architects obviously see this as a contradiction, but it merely recognises that architecture is much more than just the work of architects. Some of the most speculative and thoughtful architecture is produced by the 'illegal' architect who may, for example, also be a user, an artist or a surgeon. Consequently, a definition that threatens the profession is that architecture is not just a building, a form, a stable entity with fixed dimensions. Instead, architecture is, primarily, a particular relationship between a subject and an object, in which the former occupies the latter, which is not necessarily a building, but can be a space, text, artwork or any other phenomenon that displays, or refers to, the subject-object relationships particular to architecture. Furthermore, in architecture, there are two occupations not one—first, the activities of the designer, and, second, the actions of the user. The designer and user both make architecture. The role of the latter is as important as that of the former.

**FIGURE 15 Perspective Looking North, Production Space for Sound, Institute of Illegal Architects.** Transient Elements in the drawing: Modulator (02) Eye contact initiates a sensual response from a catalogue of muted sounds, smells, and sights. Gnome (09) An inflatable garden gnome painted in a single colour appropriate to its location, it does very little. Cleaner (21) Compensates for signs of order by dirtying the interior with an appropriate sound, sight or smell. Table (43) Formed from four materials: plastic, steel, wood and soap, each exactly the same colour—orange. Television (78) A 1960s appliance produced by Piretta in Italy specifically for indoor and outdoor use.

Between the perceived binary opposition of the didactic, prescriptive architect within the institution and passive, receptive user without is a third entity, the illegal architect who is also a user.[56] An architecture that responds to the creative unpredictability of the user is more likely to be initiated by an illegal architect than a professional one, because the former feels no antagonism towards the user. Architecture often contradicts the intentions of its designer and each user constructs a new architecture through the act of using. A profusion of ambiguities and interpretations inhabit the gap between designing and using, but this does not imply that the illegal architect should be without ideas. The illegal architect should be aware of, and indeed use, the limitations of architectural practice.[57] Instead of assuming that a drawing, model or text accurately describes architecture, it is important to recognise the differences between the one and the other as well as their similarities. For example, at one moment the abstraction of the drawing, the very fact that it is very different from the building, may be useful while, for a different purpose, it may be productive to exploit the similarities of the drawing and the building. A more knowing investigation of architectural discourse and practice would initiate a three-fold investigation of the architectural drawing. First, to consider how the drawing and architecture are similar and different; second, to develop new ways of visualising the qualities of architecture excluded from the drawing; and third, if these cannot be drawn, to find other ways to describe and discuss them.

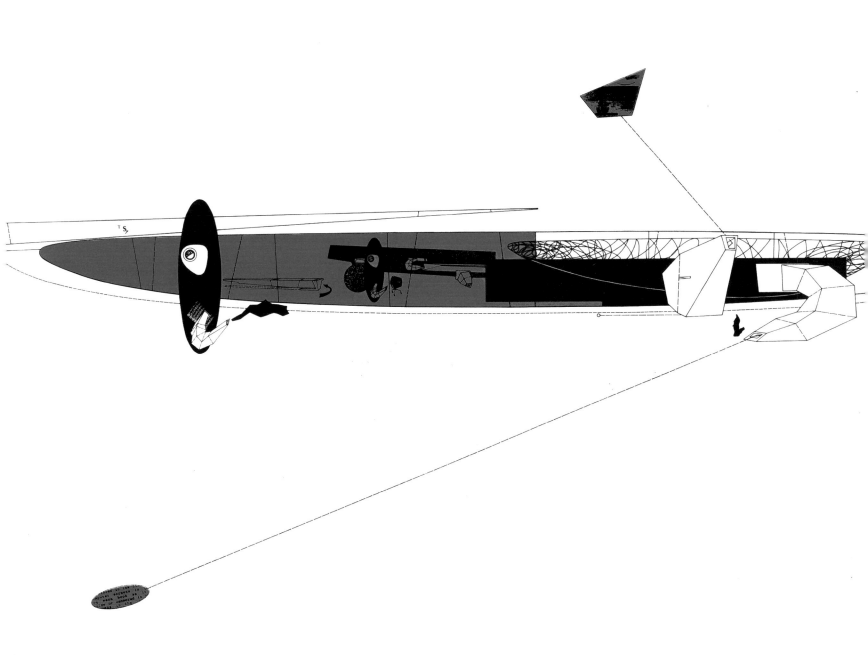

The illegal architect must couple creativity with considerable logistic and practical skills. In no way is this text a denial of the latter. Rather it argues that, at present, the profession does not encourage the co-existence of these skills. The RIBA provides this text with a tangible target, but my criticism of the architectural profession is not specific to Britain. In arguing that the unbiased expertise of the professional is rarely compatible with the committed creation of architecture, THE ILLEGAL ARCHITECT is a proposal for a different type of architectural producer, one unrestrained by professionalism. However, the illegal architect is not just a person who produces architecture without a professional qualification. The illegal architect questions and subverts the conventions, codes and 'laws' of architecture, and, therefore, can even be a registered architect critical of the profession. Implicit within this is the belief that the legal architect can learn from the illegal architect, for whom architecture can be made of anything, anywhere, anyhow, by anyone, a proposition outlined in the following pages.

The practices and materials of architecture are interdependent. It is not possible to really question one without the other. Two unfortunate consequences of the architectural profession's attempts to protect its 'territory' are isolation from developments in other cultural fields and a narrow range of procedures and materials. Architectural practice has yet to undergo a transformation analogous to the one which has been so liberating in art. Of particular relevance is the idea that art can be made of anything, which this text applies to architecture. In 1990, Jannis Kounellis exhibited, at the National Gallery in Berlin, an artwork which was also a wall, consisting of two sheets of glass in a steel frame. The void between the glass was full of coffee beans which blocked the view from one side to the other but allowed a gentle light to filter through the tiny gaps between the beans. Two distinct cultural disciplines, for example sculpture and architecture, cannot be fused into a cohesive whole because distinct forces frame each activity but, if the experience of an artwork is closer to that expected of architecture than art, it can be defined as architecture in specific ways, whether spatial, material or temporal, especially if considered as a series of strategies, elements and techniques rather than an indivisible whole.

FIGURE 16 **East Elevation, Production Space for Sound and Section, Production Space for Smell, Institute of Illegal Architects.** The Production Space for Sound balances on the Production Space for Smell. The inlet/outlet recessed into the surface of the former transforms sounds into images and projects them into the RIBA. Minute pores in the broken cracked skin of the latter allow smells to permeate between the spaces of the IIA and RIBA. Two cast iron street lamps, one outside the RIBA and the other close to the ARB, house a camera and high powered projection equipment. On rainy nights, fragments of the ARB are photographed and dissembled in the adjacent street lamp, transmitted to the one outside the RIBA and cast down into the concave surface of the Production Space for Smell. The process is repeated in reverse from the RIBA to the ARB.

Most architects would characterise a wall of coffee beans as irrelevant to architecture but fail to explain why it is unlikely that such a wall would be conceived by an architect. Architecture is perceived to be the epitome of stability and the actions of the architect must appear equally secure if they are to provide the protection expected by the state and the client. The professional is associated with a sense of propriety and the architectural materials used by architects must be equally reasonable: brick, steel, glass and concrete. A wall of coffee beans would be unlikely to be designed by an architect because it questions the sense of propriety and authority expected of a professional.

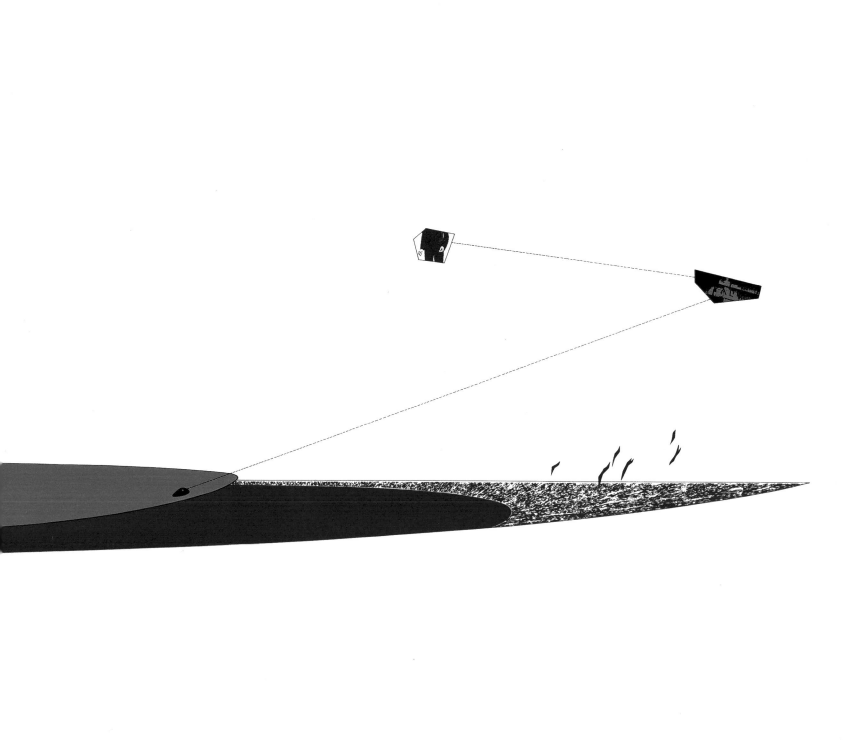

The ability to accept and enjoy instability is a sign of maturity in an individual as well as a society. It is quite different to either the obsessive desire for the new or the nostalgic preservation of the old. When architecture is a disposable toy or a preserved artefact, the user is treated as a passive consumer. Therefore, the IIA combines familiar and unfamiliar materials to suggest an unstable and incomplete architecture that is made by both the illegal architect and the active user. The aim being not to complete the building, but to enjoy its lack of completion:

> The organic work intends the impression of wholeness. To the extent its individual elements
> have significance only as they relate to the whole, they always point to the work as a whole
> as they are perceived individually. In the avant-gardiste work, on the other hand, the
> individual elements have a much higher degree of autonomy and can be read and interpreted
> individually or in groups without it being necessary to grasp the work as a whole. In the case
> of the avant-gardiste work, it is possible only to a limited extent to speak of the work as a
> whole as the perfect embodiment of the totality of possible meanings.[58]

It is fairly simple to imagine an architecture of unfamiliar materials if this presumes that architecture is only a building. Traditionally, architecture is made for a particular place. Buildings are prototypes which never go into production because the cultural, economic, political and physical conditions vary from project to project. The familiar experience of architecture is dependent upon the user being in the same time and place as the building. However, the mass-production of perception, from the printed page to the internet, has transformed the meaning of site, space, time and distance by which architecture is judged and defined.[59]

In extending the principle of technological determinism to contemporary culture, Marshall McLuhan suggests that, when one cultural form displaces another in importance, the older form either declines or changes its character to become the content of the new one.[60] In NOTRE-DAME OF PARIS, Victor Hugo said that "This will kill that. The book will kill the building.".[61] If I extend this argument further, the book killed the building, the film killed the book and the computer killed the film—each successive medium denuding the former of its role and purpose. As we place more and more human functions within the domain of the machine we may find that one day artificial intelligence supersedes human intelligence. Manuel De Landa's book WAR IN THE AGE OF INTELLIGENT MACHINES was published in

FIGURE 17 **Production Space for Smell, Institute of Illegal Architects.** At a maximum length and width of, respectively, 100 metres and 30 metres, the concave shell of the Production Space for Smell has a steel structure faced on both sides with a skin of cracked, but not broken, glass. Four metres deep at its widest point, it narrows to one metre at the rim.

the United States in 1991.[62] Assuming the persona of a robot historian, De Landa foresees the time when artificial intelligence is dominant. Maybe that day is nearer than we think, because pages 176 to 225 were deleted from my copy of De Landa's book and replaced with a repeat of the previous fifty pages. Clearly, the omitted pages were too threatening for the machine to allow their publication.

Technological determinism also appears in Jean Baudrillard's theory of sign production. Baudrillard identifies three distinct historical periods, or orders, in the development of sign production since the fifteenth century. In the counterfeit stage, from the Renaissance to industrialisation, the form of the commodity was personified by the stucco angel: a single copy from a 'natural' original. In the production stage, industrialisation generated the serial equivalence of objects copied from an original. Finally, in the simulation stage of contemporary culture, Baudrillard identifies the endless circulation of signs without origin.

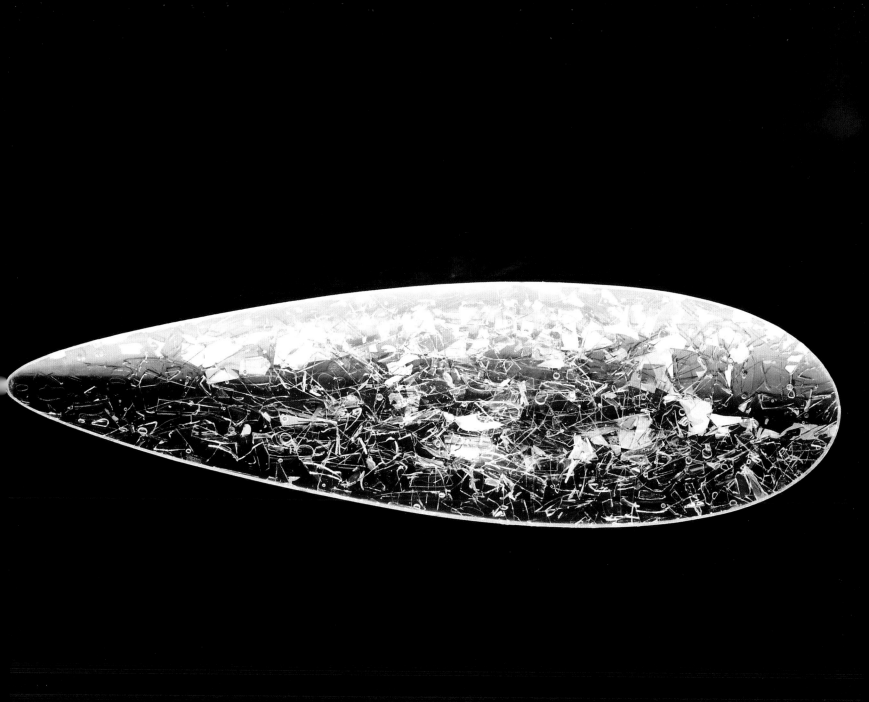

McLuhan and Baudrillard describe linear histories in which one form of technology or sign production supersedes another and the sites and spaces of architecture are transformed as its importance is progressively diminished. However, contemporary architecture is characterised by multiple sites, such as the building, book, gallery, film, and computer, and overlapping spatial conditions, whether perspectival, cinematic, or virtual. Rather than a progression from one form to another, the sites and spaces of architecture accumulate in complex hybrids. For example, film and virtual reality still use Renaissance perspective, while the computer employs early twentieth century montage. Consequently, we should not talk about the site, space and experience of architecture but the sites, spaces and experiences of architecture.

In searching for authors, materials, sites and practices outside the conventional boundaries of the discipline, THE ILLEGAL ARCHITECT also suggests a larger agenda which defines architecture in primarily spatial terms. Two ideas, the linearity of thought and the primacy of form, perhaps condition the development of architecture more than any other. But, as ephemerality and speed of change are two of the most distinctive qualities of the contemporary city, space may be more tangible than a line and more solid than a form. This conception of space, as a physical but fluid presence, inverts the conventional understanding of architectural space as the void between material, tangible elements: the walls, floors and ceilings. Space is usually classified in two ways, as a perceptual phenomenon and an intellectual process.[63] For illegal architects, the aim must be to design space and to think spatially, suggesting a spatiality of product as well as process. The former has a fairly clear meaning. The latter is a more complex proposition. By this I mean the ability to make unexpected non-linear connections between diverse phenomena. A few years ago, I overheard a conversation between a biologist and a physicist. The physicist said to the biologist: "You've got to have a model.". The biologist replied to the physicist: "But I am a biologist. We evolve things. It might end up as a golden eagle or a wart hog.". Obviously, I am on the side of the biologist. Thinking in spatial terms enables us to learn from all the work around us, not just that produced by architects. Applied to architecture, the spatiality of cultural production suggests a series of distinct but dependent procedures, so that the form, site and materials

FIGURE 18 Detail of Cracked Glass Skin, Production Space for Smell, Institute of Illegal Architects.

of a project are selected because they are appropriate not merely expected. The materials of a project may, for example, be ice and steel, or soap and stone, while the illegal architect can be a musician, the project an experiment and the site an operating theatre.

The history, design and use of architecture can be re-conceived through the adoption of a spatial model for each activity. Most systems of thought adopt the hierarchical model of a tree in which a leaf is traced to the roots via the branch and trunk. Probably the most obvious example of linearity occurs in the conventional understanding of history in which the past leads (logically) to the present.

The cliché that we can objectively study the past but not the present is a curious idea, as our experience of one is far more detailed than of the other. The past is not a fixed point to which we can return and experience 'as it really was'. Maybe it only seems to be clearer because it is easier to edit the information. Certainly, there is a type of historian who is only happy if the object of his analysis does not wriggle (i.e. is dead).

The Barcelona Pavilion was built for an exhibition in 1929 and dismantled in the same year. About ten years ago it was rebuilt with the help of photographs.[64] So how old is the Pavilion? Is it an historical monument, a copy of an original, or a new building? The past is always made in the present and continuously re-made to suit the present. Histories are never neutral, they are provisional, selective and ideological. "For every image of the past that is not recognised by the present as one of its own concerns threatens to disappear irretrievably."[65]

It is normal for an historical text to be structured chronologically. But what if history is spatial rather than linear? An event in 1998 may be closer to one in 1923 than another in 1992. Instead of a model of historical progression, I suggest one of oscillating spatial flux in which change does not happen simply in a linear sequence. The film BLADE RUNNER presents a convincing allegory for the spatiality of history in which umbrellas exist alongside futuristic machines and the narrator is both a Chandleresque detective and an android assassin.[66] A spatial understanding of history suggests that, for example, Modernism and Post-Modernism are not distinct historical moments. Instead, they are sets of opposed theories and values present throughout the twentieth century in a continuous and parallel process of dependence and confrontation. Consequently, many artists and architects can be categorised as both Modernist and Post-Modernist. While Alvar Aalto developed contradictions within one project, Le Corbusier developed contradictory projects within one architect.

**FIGURE 19 Elevation of Internal Wall, Production Space for Smell, Institute of Illegal Architects.** Clear glass storage containers are set into the opaque glass internal walls within the Production Space for Smell. Each container holds a specific raw material before it is removed and its essence extracted. Each container has a measuring scale specific to the scale and volume of its contents. As the containers empty and fill, the degree of transparency in a wall is transformed, so that the framed is more solid than the frame and vice versa.

Another division to consider is the one between the architect and the historian. The architectural profession claims a monopoly over architectural design for the purpose of economic and social self-protection. Although unregulated by the law, the architectural historian claims a similar monopoly within the field of history. Architects and architectural historians monitor and patrol their domains to exclude critics from within and intruders from without, including each other. In the architectural text, the antagonism between the architect and the historian is usually translated into a fight between the theorist and the historian, in which the latter implies that theory is subjective and history objective. But this conceals that history is theory. In refuting the disciplinary autonomy of the historian and the architect, connections between the text and building can be explored by the same person without the false division of theory, history and design.

—9

—5
—4
—3

0·8 —
0·6 —
0·4 —
0·2 —

—6

—50
—25

—30
—20

—2000

—0·3

—150
—100
—50

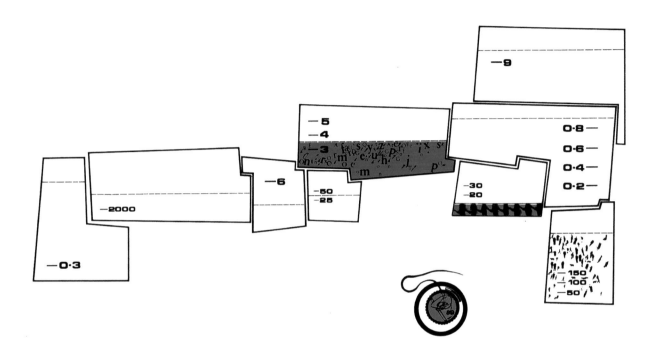

To replace linearity with spatiality would, however, be ineffective if one system were simply exchanged for another. Instead I am interested in a spatiality of thought and design that moves from the absurd linearity found in two strategies of Surrealism, the Paranoid Critical Method and Exquisite Corpse, to a three-dimensional spatial montage which is a hybrid of the linear and spatial. The Paranoid Critical Method (PCM) is a strategy, devised by Salvador Dali, in which a chance decision is pursued to the limits of its logic. It is both rational and irrational, a combination that confuses and even invalidates the two categories. The PCM is so tantalising and rewarding because its logic is fearless. As Rem Koolhaas states: "The paranoiac always hits the nail on the head, no matter where the hammer blows fall.".[67] The PCM questions the conventions of authorship because the author of an idea becomes the servant of that idea. Consequently, the most important time to proceed is the point when the creator of the process most wants to stop. This is a moment of infinite pain and pleasure: when the idea, now a project, questions the prejudices of its author.

In 1978, Koolhaas published DELIRIOUS NEW YORK. Sub-titling the book A RETROACTIVE MANIFESTO FOR MANHATTAN, the author presented an alternative history of Modernism, one driven by the surreal rationality which he found in the PCM. However, in 1936 Dali was expelled from the Surrealist movement, in part because his creative process displayed only the illusion of chance.[68] It is equally possible to see Koolhaas' use of the PCM as not an alternative to Functionalism but as Functionalism taken to extremes: "... the inner workings of the Paranoid Critical Method: limp, unprovable conjectures generated through the deliberate simulation of paranoiac thought processes, supported (made critical) by the 'crutches' of Cartesian rationality.".[69]

To avoid it becoming merely the mimic of rationalism, the PCM must be used not once but many times: as a tool for experimentation in which the critical intellect is reintroduced at the end of each 'journey', so that a field of investigation and its architecture is gradually defined within a spider's web of multiple journeys. One 'play' of the PCM may concern an important material, another use, another a means of representation, another weather, another a practice from outside architecture. Each separate play of the PCM has to be pushed to the limit of its logic before it is compared to, and combined with, the others.

FIGURE 20 Visual Index of the Transient Elements, Institute of Illegal Architects.

The Exquisite Corpse shifts the emphasis from the single author to hybrid author-readers who both make and consume a work. It is a game played by several people, who compose a sentence without anyone seeing the preceding collaborations, each player in turn writing a word or phrase before folding the paper to conceal their contribution and passing it on to the next player. André Breton stated that: "... with 'Exquisite Corpse' we had at our disposal—at last—an infallible means of temporarily dismissing the critical mind and of fully freeing metaphorical activity.".[70] The first sentence produced by the game created its name: "The exquisite corpse will drink the new wine.".[71] It is more familiarly known as a children's game in which, instead of the words of a sentence, each participant draws a part of the body, first the head, then the neck, torso, waist, legs and feet. In the IIA, the Exquisite Corpse is used as a strategy with which to juxtapose objects and events. In addition to the five spatial zones, the IIA contains a collection of Transient Elements, the number and character of which are in a constant state of flux. The rules for the combination of the Transient Elements refer to the Exquisite Corpse but, instead of the linearity of the Surrealist game, the Transient Elements relate to each other spatially. Each Element 'does something', some functions are obvious, others are not. Juxtapositions are determined by the users not the designer.

The Exquisite Corpse is a form of montage, which is both a technical and an artistic procedure. As the former, montage is the method of assembly used in industrial mass-production and in film. As the latter, it is the principal technique of the twentieth century avant-garde. Montage, as a non-organic form of art, proclaims its artificiality and opposes the organic work of art, which obscures its artificiality. In the organic work of art, the individual parts are subordinate to, and in harmony with, the overall composition while, in the non-organic work of art, the parts, setting and context are in contradiction with each other. Montage deploys all the techniques of allegory: the depletion of meaning, the fragmentation and dialectical juxtaposition of parts and their dissemination through a new context. The uneasy resolution of montage indicates that meaning is historically contingent, open to revision, and cultural rather than natural. It opposes the mythical autonomies of culture and can directly engage in ideologies and modes of representation outside the confines of a discipline through the appropriation of procedures and images taken from the world as a whole.

Walter Benjamin used montage to discuss montage. It is both the subject, method and form of the unfinished PASSAGENWERK, his study of the nineteenth-century Parisian arcades. Benjamin suggested that, although industrialisation had produced a fragmentation of experience and perception, it had also, through the invention of film, created the means by which the world could be comprehended and reconstructed because the montage of experiences is the essential structure of film and the contemporary world. He believed that the advent of mechanical reproduction would free art from its dependence on ritual and tradition, transforming it from the representation of myths to the analysis of illusions.[72] However, the consequences of montage were overstated by Benjamin and it is equally possible to question its relevance as a critical and creative tool now that it is the excepted strategy of art and advertising. I agree with both points if montage is only used as a means to construct visual or textual juxtapositions. However, I am interested in the gaps in a montage as well as the juxtapositions. The work of two artists and one architect, Laszlo Moholy-Nagy, John Baldessari and Mies van der Rohe, indicate the form of three-dimensional spatial montage I am advocating, in which the gaps are even more important than the elements.[73]

FIGURE 21 Textual Index of the Transient Elements, Institute of Illegal Architects.

All three use absence, the sense of something missing, to ensure that the viewer or occupant has a constructive role in the formulation of a work. Montage is often associated with the shock tactics of the avant-garde, which are now too familiar to evoke much surprise. A montage of gaps and absences would not be shocking and then acceptable, but remain unresolved, to be continually re-made by each user. Architecture by accident rather than design.[74]

**02 MODULATOR**
Eye contact initiates a sensual response from a range of muted sounds, smells and sights

**06 REFLECTOR**
Images of the RIBA and the ARB are projected into reflectors recessed into the street

**09 GNOME**
An inflatable garden gnome painted in a single colour appropriate to its location, it does very little

**11 FLOOR**
A pressure-sensitive rubber panel activates a field of white noise of variable intensity

**13 SUITCASE**
The travelling case houses slide projection equipment, a microphone and speakers

**14 CARAVAN**
Painted white with blue lilac trim and tartan upholstery, it sleeps four very comfortably

**15 SOFA**
Upholstered in blue lycra, the sofa becomes softer as it reaches its maximum length of 70 m

**17 KITCHEN**
An oven and freezer are housed within a corrugated steel box and marble fireplace

**18 ARCHITECT**
White, male, heterosexual and presumed to be dead, he trusts in reincarnation

**21 CLEANER**
Compensates for signs of order by dirtying a space with an appropriate sound, sight or smell

**22 NOZZLES**
The four dispersal and suction nozzles are recessed into the pivoting door at the main entrance

**25 SHAFT**
The surface of the shaft is progressively encased in compressed workshop debris

**29 SHADOW**
Shadows in the RIBA are constructed as three-dimensional resin forms in the IIA

**32 WHEEL**
Connected to a sliding door, it activates spectacolor slits concealed in the floor

**42 CLOCK**
The IIA is open twenty four hours a day, three hundred and sixty five days a year

**43 TABLE**
Formed of four materials: plastic, steel, wood and soap, each exactly the same colour: orange

**44 WASHER**
A manual operation washing machine, it rotates at a speed of 12.5 spins a minute

**45 FRAME**
Used for scaling, it contains a glass door that can be looked through but not opened

**47 COMPUTER**
Monitors in the IIA log each book as it is banned, stolen or censored in the RIBA

**55 CHAIR**
A clone of transient element 15, it is divided into sections and located wherever necessary

**56 TIMELOCK**
Located next to the entrance to the shared toilets of the RIBA and IIA, it does not work

**67 DUCT**
It magnifies the sounds, sights and smells of the IIA and projects them into the RIBA

**68 AUTOMOBILE**
A 1956 pink Chevrolet Corvette with red upholstery, it seats four for drive-in movies

**76 ANGEL**
Cast in concrete, it is set into a glass wall in which the framed is more solid than the frame

**78 TELEVISION**
A 1960s model produced by Piretta in Italy specifically for indoor and outdoor use

**80 FAN**
Activated by eye contact, it operates at a number of speeds but is always totally silent

**83 CHAISE**
Made at various lengths, its softness and lack of armrests invites contact between occupants

**85 STORE**
Pigment, seed and polystyrene are mixed in the store and dispersed by the nozzles

**87 MIRROR**
A mirror with a broken glass frame, the former magnifies by four, the latter reduces by two

**88 PERISCOPE**
It transfers sights, sounds and smells from the interior to the exterior and vice versa

In addition to space being perceived and conceived, it is also lived in. That the illegal architect should consider how space is occupied is one of the major themes of this text.[75] It is more common for architects to discuss forms and functions than spaces and accidents.[76] The interest in form rather than space is reinforced by the photograph. The reputation of an architect is now largely dependent on his or her ability to generate a good photograph. If an architect is 'successful' the same image is published throughout the world, to be copied by other architects with little regard to cultural or social differences. An emphasis on form and the photograph reduces architecture to a primarily visual phenomenon. Form is, primarily, produced for, and occupied by, the eye while space is inhabited in more subtle and sensual ways.

Function appears in numerous texts, but accidents are hardly discussed at all. In this century, the question of how architecture is occupied is often answered with function, suggesting that a snug fit between form and function is desirable. The two most common alternatives either suggest the opposite, that form should follow function, or propose a bland definition of architecture in which anything can happen and nothing actually does. Many theories of architecture assume a master-servant relationship between form and function, with one leading and the other following, but architecture is rarely so simple. A door handle has a very limited range of uses, a bed many more.

Whether the discussion is phrased in positive or negative terms, function and use are more often linked to pragmatism than pleasure, with which they have an uneasy relationship. Modernists tend to assume that visual beauty is a product of function. The degree of pleasure, if it can be called that, derived from a form being in direct proportion to its efficiency for a task. Bernard Tschumi has suggested the opposite, that pleasure is derived from the mis-use of form, while many of the more famous contemporary architects assume that the pleasure of a form is independent of its function.[77] The architectural profession's trivialisation of pleasure is a fundamental error that ignores the mechanisms of desire essential to use. Pleasure and love are still not respectable subjects for architecture. Most theories of architecture allude to rationality, which by implication denies and demeans pleasure. Of course, if we try to understand love, we may miss the point.[78] Space is particularly seductive

FIGURE 22 Production Space for Touch, Institute of Illegal Architects. The Production Space for Touch is located below Portland Place, underneath the Production Space for Time and the glass shell of the Production Space for Smell. It has a blue light-box floor aligned with the level of the water-table under London. A wide timber ramp leads up to the Production Space for Sight. A circular glazed opening in the surface of the street is placed above the mirror wall at each end of the space. Aligned at 45° to the floor, the mirrors enable a pedestrian in Portland Place to look along the length of the Production Space for Touch without entering it and to observe another person doing the same.

because it is so hard to grasp and define. "We make a vessel from a lump of clay; it is the empty space within the vessel that makes it useful. We make doors and windows for a room; thus while the tangible has advantages; it is the intangible that makes it useful."[79]

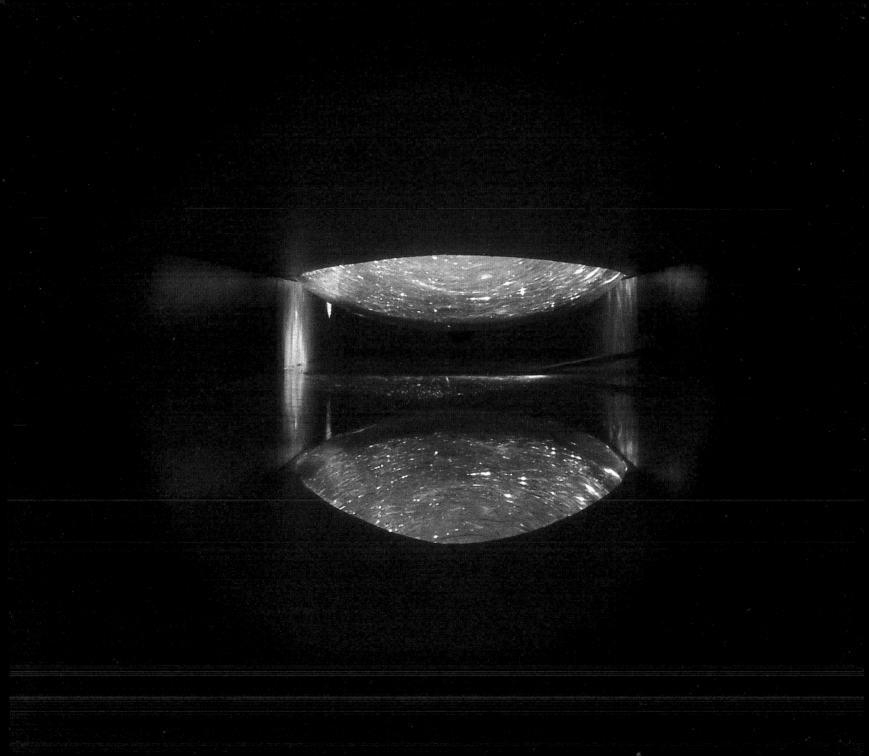

It is possible to equate Lao Tsu's statement with the conventional under-standing of architectural space as the void between solid boundaries "... in which anything can happen and nothing actually does". However, Lao Tsu's evocation of the intangibility of space also suggests something quite different. Maybe the majority of architecture is prosaic because it is so obviously architecture. Paradoxically, the most suggestive architecture maybe the one we do not know how to occupy. The concept of incompletion implicit in Lao Tsu's statement suggests an architecture of shifting spatial and semantic gaps so that, rather than empty, a space is waiting to be filled. In speaking about the education at the architecture school of the Illinois Institute of Technology in the 1950s James Ingo Freed states the opposite to Lao Tsu: "At that time, we were made to feel the tangibility of space, we could swim in it; like a fish swims in water. Space was a metaphysical solid. You didn't have to confine yourself to the surface of a wall to imbue a building with symbolism; space itself had iconic and symbolic value.".[80]

Lao Tsu and Freed suggest, in a limited way, one of the most important qualities of space: that it is made not found. Consequently, there are many fluid spaces not a single static one. Space is seductive precisely because it is a complex combination of the tangible and intangible. The most creative occupations of architecture occur neither in a building with an obvious nor an undefined use, but in the one in which the accidents of space are at their most seductive. The ice rink is such a place. In films it is often the site of a romantic encounter. How often have we seen two characters in a film fall over and proceed to fall in love in each other's arms. The luminosity and slipperiness of the surface, the particular reverberation of sound and the sheer abundance of space loosen the familiar codes of behaviour. "This relation can, of course, be continuous and logical (the skater skates on the skating rink), but it can also be unlikely and incompatible (e.g. the quarter-back tangoes on the skating rink; the battalion skates on the tightrope)."[81]

FIGURE 23 Perspective, the Production Space for Touch, Institute of Illegal Architects. The Service Shaft connects the Production Spaces for Touch, Smell, and Sound. It is hung from the underside of the concave elliptical glass shell of the Production Space for Smell but does not quite touch the light-box floor of the Production Space for Touch. The surface of the shaft is encased in compressed workshop debris. The shaft expands by two millimetres per hour as the waste accumulates. Transient Elements in the drawing: Modulator (02) Eye contact initiates a sensual response from a catalogue of muted sounds, smells, and sights. Gnome (09) An inflatable garden gnome painted in a single colour appropriate to its location, it does very little. Cleaner (21) Compensates for signs of order by dirtying the interior with a selected sound, sight or smell. Television (78) A 1960s appliance produced by Piretta in Italy specifically for indoor and outdoor use.

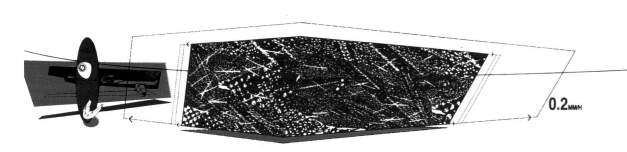

0.2мм/ч

Many of the qualities of space I describe occur in a border. Although it is normally assumed to be a line, a border actually has a thickness and edges. Often the edges of a border are monitored but not its centre, which is not recognised and defined to the same extent as the territories to each side of it. So often we assume a place is empty, when it is actually full of what we do not see. A border is not a void, rather it is a liminal space. The manner in which a person crosses or occupies a border informs its effect upon them.

Set half a metre forward of the Portland Place elevation of the RIBA are two columns, one either side of the entrance. Each column is surmounted by a sculpted figure dedicated to the 'creative forces in architecture'.[82] Turned towards each other but with their faces angled to the sky and bodies slightly crouched, the figure on the left is female, the one on the right is male. An individual entering the RIBA passes between the two columns, which imply that an equality of the sexes exists within the building. However, the single sculpture of a female figure is outnumbered by the numerous male figures on the facades, just as there are far more male than female members of the RIBA. Underneath the columns, the basement of the RIBA extends a little over a metre beyond the line of the front elevation. Beneath the column with the female figure are the female toilets and beneath the column with the male figure are the male toilets. In the hierarchical but accidental juxtaposition of design and defecation, the RIBA appears to mock itself, the higher values to which it alludes resting on more everyday human concerns.

In the National Museum of Modern Art at the Pompidou Centre, Paris, the toilets are deposited adjacent to the art in portacabin-like capsules, a strategy reminiscent of both Duchamp and Manzoni. Forty years after Duchamp produced FOUNTAIN, Manzoni labelled, numbered and signed ninety cans of MERDA D'ARTISTA, each filled with 30 grams of the artist's excrement. The distance between the columns and the toilets at the RIBA is similar to that between the art and toilets at the Pompidou but, while the former are located one above the other and separated by a concrete pavement, the latter are side by side and spatially connected. The blurring of art and life is one of the principal themes of twentieth century art and there is a temptation to view the toilets at the Pompidou as yet another rather fashionable, if unintended, art installation. However, they also

**FIGURE 24** Perspective, Glass Sliding Wall Leading to the Shared Toilets, The Production Space for Touch, The Institute of Illegal Architects. Cast concrete cylinders are set within the glass sliding side wall which leads from the IIA to the shared toilets in the basement of the RIBA, so that the framed is more solid than the frame. Two periscopes set within the sliding wall juxtapose the sounds of the toilets with those of the spaces to each side. Transient Elements in the drawing: Cleaner (21) Compensates for signs of order by dirtying the interior with an appropriate sound, sight or smell. Table (43) Formed from four materials: plastic, steel, wood and soap, each exactly the same colour—orange.

suggest a relaxed attitude to the functioning of bodily behaviour, art and architecture. Seemingly the most functionally delineated of spaces, toilets can also be the most domestic and intimate: the site of events and conversations impossible in the other spaces of a public building. The only physical connection between the RIBA and the IIA leads from the toilets in the basement of the former to the Production Space for Touch in the lowest level of the latter. The toilets are shared by the two institutes but are no longer gendered. In the most prosaic of spaces, both border and toilet, the professional and illegal architect meet and cross over into each other's spaces.

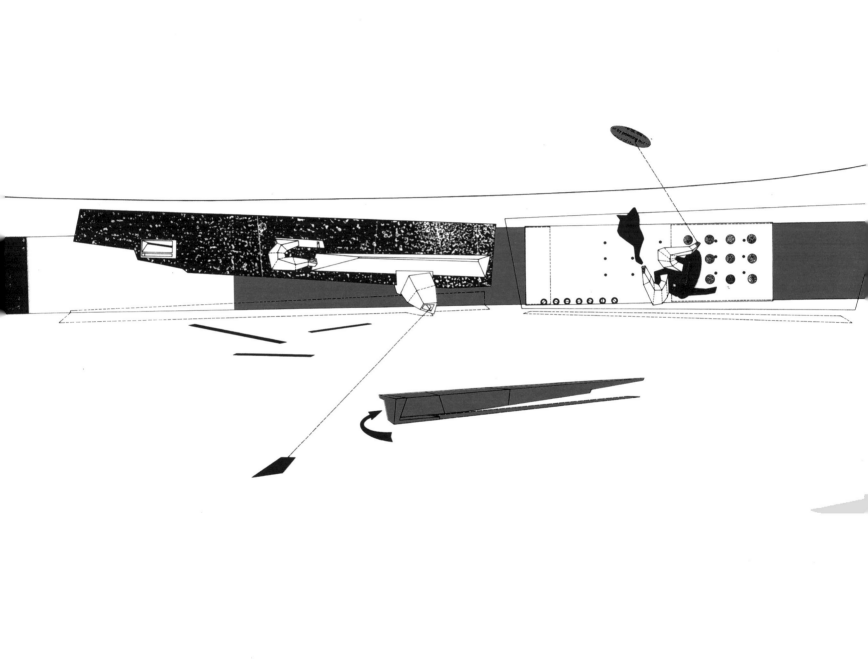

# NOTES

1. It is common for a specific institution, and institution itself as a concept, to be the subject of simultaneous attack. However, the avant-garde denial of the institutions of art and architecture at the beginning of the century collapsed on the myth of its own anti-institutionalism, resulting in either the withering away of radical practice or the incorporation of its de-politicised husk within an expanded discipline. In accepting the original principles of avant-gardism, so many of the seemingly radical projects produced in the last few years have concentrated on the minor. However, marginality and the role of the outsider are self-fulfilling. Institutions must be formed or re-formed not destroyed. They are essential to the advocacy of change.

2. G. Grey Wornum won the competition to design the building in May 1932. Margaret Richardson, 66 PORTLAND PLACE: THE LONDON HEADQUARTERS OF THE ROYAL INSTITUTE OF BRITISH ARCHITECTS, London: RIBA Publications Limited, 1984, p. 4.

3. The manual skills of the artisan and mechanic are devalued within the class system. The practice of the professional is perceived to be of a higher order because it is intellectual rather than physical labour.

4. R. Dingwall and P. Lewis (eds.), THE SOCIOLOGY OF THE PROFESSIONS: LAWYERS, DOCTORS AND OTHERS, London: The Macmillan Press, 1983, p. 5. See also Katerina Rüedi, "Curriculum Vitæ. The Architect's Cultural Capital: Educational Practices and Financial Investments", in Jonathan Hill (ed.), OCCUPYING ARCHITECTURE: BETWEEN THE ARCHITECT AND THE USER, London: Routledge, forthcoming 1998.

5. Peter Bürger, THEORY OF THE AVANT-GARDE, Manchester, Manchester University Press, 1985, p. 46.

6. It is of course possible to classify art as an industry of mass-production and mass-consumption. It is certainly the latter if not the former. It is also questionable whether art now has more 'autonomy' than any other form of work.

7. Alexander Tzonis and Liane Lefaivre, "The Question Of Autonomy in Architecture", THE HARVARD ARCHITECTURE REVIEW, Vol. 3, Winter 1984, pp. 27 – 43.

8. Henri Lefebvre, THE PRODUCTION OF SPACE, trans. Donald Nicholson-Smith, Oxford: Blackwell, 1991, p. 89.

9. Bürger, THEORY, p. 25.

10. The denial of utility is equally important.

11. The relationship of the architecture school to the profession is complex as they are antagonistic towards, and dependent upon, each other.

12. The boundary between the two disciplines is however confused as architecture is an art but rarely a fine art.

13. Bürger, THEORY, pp. 47 – 54.

14. Regent's Park was designed by John Nash in 1811 for the Prince Regent, after whom it is named. The park is the culmination of a route which begins at Carlton House Terrace in the Mall, where the Prince Regent lived, proceeds north to Regent Street, Portland Place and then Park Crescent.

15. Philip Tabor, "Striking Home: The Telematic assault on Identity", in Hill, ARCHITECTURE.

16. Financial status is now as crucial.

17. Roman Jakobson, "Dear Claude, Cher Maître", in Marshall Blonsky (ed.) ON SIGNS, Oxford: Basil Blackwell, 1985, p. 185.

18. Lesley Lokko, Diploma Unit 12 Programme, The Bartlett School of Architecture, University College London, 1995.

19. Pierre Bourdieu, OUTLINE OF A THEORY OF PRACTICE, Cambridge: Cambridge University Press, 1991, pp. 171 – 183.

20. For a discussion of Bourdieu's theory of cultural capital and its relation to the architect see Rüedi, in Hill, ARCHITECTURE.

21. Rosa Prince, "What do Labour's new MPs think?", RIBA JOURNAL, September 1997, Vol. 104, No. 9, p. 13.

22. In 1996, I proposed an Institute of Architecture, rather than one of architects. The RIBA is considering a change of name, possibly to the Royal Institute of British Architecture. However, this would be no change at all, and would emphasise the existing principles of the institute, unless the criteria for membership were expanded, the management of the institute taken out of the hands of architects and the role of the ARB transformed.

23. Lefebvre, SPACE, p. 89.

24. Accidents do happen, of course, whether fortuitous or not.

25. Elizabeth Wright, PSYCHOANALYTIC CRITICISM: THEORY IN PRACTICE, London: Routledge, 1984, p. 93.

26. Mary McLeod, "Architecture or Revolution: Taylorism, Technocracy and Social Change", ART JOURNAL, No. 43: 2, Summer 1983, pp. 132 – 147.

27. Determinism assumes that every event has a cause.

28. Le Corbusier's Modulor being one. Tony Vidler, "The Building in Pain", AA FILES, No. 19, 1991, p. 3.

29. Edward De Zurko, ORIGINS OF FUNCTIONALIST THEORY, New York: Columbia University Press, 1957.

30. Le Corbusier, TOWARDS A NEW ARCHITECTURE, London: Rodker, 1927, p. 10.

31. The less photographed rear elevation suggests that the sanatorium can also be understood as a montage. Demetri Porphyrios, SOURCES OF MODERN ECLECTICISM: STUDIES ON ALVAR AALTO, London: Academy Editions, 1982.

32. Beatriz Colomina, "The Split Wall: Domestic Voyeurism", in Beatriz Colomina (ed.), SEXUALITY AND SPACE, New York: Princeton Architectural Press, 1992, pp. 73 – 130.

33. Colomina, "Domestic", p. 75.

34. Colomina, "Domestic", p. 98.

35. Walter Benjamin, "The Work of Art in Age of Mechanical Reproduction", in Hannah Arendt (ed.), WALTER BENJAMIN: ILLUMINATIONS, trans. Harry Zohn, New York: Schocken Books, 1969, pp. 217 – 252. In identifying self-understanding as the purpose of art in Bourgeois society, Bürger has suggested that art was separated from praxis so that the former could redeem the sense of individuality lost in the latter. Bürger, THEORY, p. 48.

36. A number of arts, such as music and film, are experienced in different ways to Gallery art. However, the experience of architecture is more often discussed in terms appropriate to Gallery art than music, film or even architecture.

37. Colomina, "Domestic".

38. The term 'user' is problematic because it can be coupled with pragmatism and rationality or even drug addiction. However, it is a more appropriate than occupant, occupier or inhabitant because it implies both positive action and the potential for abuse and mis-use.

39. Donna Haraway, SIMIANS, CYBORGS AND WOMEN, London: Free Association Books, 1991, Roland Barthes, "The Death of the Author", IMAGE-MUSIC-TEXT, trans. Stephen Heath, London: Flamingo, 1977, pp. 142 – 148 and Brian Willis (ed.) ROCK MY RELIGION / DAN GRAHAM, Cambridge, Mass.: MIT Press, 1993.

40. For example, in the work of Hans Haacke or James Turrell.

41. For example, Yves Klein's FIRE WALL AND FIRE FOUNTAIN, Museum Haus Lange, Krefeld, 1961.

42. Haraway, WOMEN, p. 150.

**43.** For example, Jean Baudrillard, "The Ecstacy of Communication", in Hal Foster (ed.), POST-MODERN CULTURE, London: Pluto, 1985, pp. 126 – 136 and Alberto Perez-Gomez, ARCHITECTURE AND THE CRISIS OF MODERN SCIENCE, Cambridge, Mass.: MIT Press, 1983.

**44.** Walter Benjamin, THE ORIGIN OF GERMAN TRAGIC DRAMA, trans. J. Osborne, London: New Left Books, 1977 and Dawn Ades, "Dada and Surrealism", in Nikos Stangos (ed.), CONCEPTS OF MODERN ART, London: Thames and Hudson, 1981, pp. 110 – 137.

**45.** Barthes uses writer or scriptor rather than author and refers to the example of Mallarmé. Barthes, "Author", p. 143.

**46.** Here I am using 'building' to stand for a whole range of architectural 'objects', an argument that is developed later in this text.

**47.** Hannah Arendt, "Introduction, Walter Benjamin: 1892 – 1940", in Arendt, ILLUMINATIONS, p. 24.

**48.** This story was related to the author by a Chinese citizen born and educated in Shanghai.

**49** Samuel Beckett, quoted in Brian Massumi, A USER'S GUIDE TO CAPITALISM AND SCHIZOPHRENIA, Cambridge, Mass.: MIT Press, 1992, p. 47.

**50.** "Architecture has always represented the prototype of a work of art the reception of which is consummated by a collectivity in a state of distraction." Walter Benjamin, in Arendt, ILLUMINATIONS, p. 239.

**51.** Stan Allen, "Dazed and Confused", ASSEMBLAGE, 27, 1995, p. 48.

**52.** Mark Cousins, "Building an Architect", in Hill, ARCHITECTURE.

**53.** David Sibley, GEOGRAPHIES OF EXCLUSION, London: Routledge, 1995, p. 8.

**54.** Franz Meyer, "Marfa", in Volker Rattenmeyer and Renate Petzinger (eds.), ART + DESIGN: DONALD JUDD, Stuttgart: Cantz, 1993, p. 33.

**55.** It is possible to argue that a weak discipline, even more than a strong one, requires the protection of the professional. However, a profession is compatible with a strong discipline but not a weak one because the professional denies the value of subjectivity which is essential in the latter.

**56.** Ben Godber suggests this figure is the 'knowing and subverting reader'. Ben Godber, "The Knowing and Subverting Reader", in Hill, ARCHITECTURE.

**57.** The relevance of these words to both literature and architecture emphasises the similarities of the two disciplines.

**58.** Bürger, THEORY, pp. 72 – 73.

**59.** As defined by Manfredo Tafuri, this process is linked to the 'Project of Modernity' which has its origins in the aesthetic, social and technical innovations of the fifteenth and sixteenth centuries. Tafuri links the Renaissance to the Enlightenment, Industrial Revolution and Functionalism, because they share a scientifically inspired 'modernising' agenda. Manfredo Tafuri, ARCHITECTURE AND UTOPIA: DESIGN AND CAPITALIST DEVELOPMENT, Cambridge, Mass.: MIT Press, 1980.

**60.** Marshall McLuhan, UNDERSTANDING MEDIA: THE EXTENSIONS OF MAN, New York: McGraw Hill, 1964.

**61.** Victor Hugo, NÔTRE DAME DE PARIS, trans. John Sturrock, London: Penguin, 1978, p. 186.

**62.** Manuel De Landa, WAR IN THE AGE OF INTELLIGENT MACHINES, New York: Swerve Editions, 1991.

**63.** A subtler understanding of space, as perceived, conceived and lived, is posited by Lefebvre in THE PRODUCTION OF SPACE.

64. Designed by Mies van der Rohe as the German Pavilion for the Barcelona International Exposition of 1929, the pavilion was reconstructed by Ignasi de Solà Morales, Christian Cirici and Fernando Ramos in 1986.

65. Walter Benjamin, "Theses on the Philosophy of History", in Arendt, ILLUMINATIONS, p. 255.

66. Ridley Scott (dir.) BLADE RUNNER, Warner, Ladd, Blade Runner Partnership, 1982.

67. Rem Koolhaas, DELIRIOUS NEW YORK. A RETROACTIVE MANIFESTO FOR MANHATTAN, Rotterdam: 010 Publishers, 1994, p. 238.

68. Ades, in Stangos (ed.), CONCEPTS, p. 132.

69. Koolhaas, DELIRIOUS, p. 236.

70. André Breton quoted in J. Marcel (ed.), AUTOBIOGRAPHY OF SURREALISM, New York: Viking, 1980, p. 222.

71. Breton, SURREALISM, p. 220.

72. Walter Benjamin, "The Work of Art in the Age of Mechanical Reproduction", in Arendt, ILLUMINATIONS, p. 224

73. Mies van der Rohe may seem an unusual choice but the use of montage is clear in his drawings. Mies van der Rohe, DRAWINGS FROM THE COLLECTION OF THE MUSEUM OF MODERN ART, NEW YORK, New York: The Museum of Modern Art, 1969.

74. Architecture by accident is a term suggested to me by Dr. Philip Tabor.

75. This relates both to Lefebvre's conceptualisation of social space as perceived, conceived and lived and Soja's understanding of a 'thirdspace' between and within the material and mental conceptions of space. Lefebvre, Space and Edward W. Soja, THIRDSPACE: JOURNEYS TO LOS ANGELES AND OTHER REAL AND IMAGINED PLACES, Cambridge, Mass. and Oxford: Blackwell, 1996.

76. If not as prevalent as form in architectural practice, space has an important place in the histories of twentieth century architecture.

77. Bernard Tschumi, THE MANHATTAN TRANSCRIPTS, London: Academy, 1994, p. 11. The work of Co-op Himmelb(l)au is an example of this attitude.

78. The assumption here is that pleasure and love are distinct but related.

79. Lao Tsu, quoted in Cornelius van der Ven, SPACE IN ARCHITECTURE, Amsterdam: Van Gorcum Assen, 1978, p. 3. The quote derives from Lao Tsu, TAO TE CHING, c. 550 B.C., Ch. 1, Bk. 1. Translations of this text differ. I have used the one in SPACE AND ARCHITECTURE as it is particularly architectural.

80. James Ingo Freed, quoted in B. Diamonstein, AMERICAN ARCHITECTURE NOW, New York: Rizzoli, 1985, p. 93.

81. Tschumi, TRANSCRIPTS, p. 11

82. Richardson, ROYAL, p. 18.

# ACKNOWLEDGMENTS

## CREDITS

**MODEL**
Bradley Starkey

**PHOTOGRAPHS**
**Cover**
Detail, Stuart Laidlaw and Mike Halliwell.

**FIGURE 1**
Components, Institute of Illegal Architects.
Stuart Laidlaw and Mike Halliwell.

**FIGURE 2**
Component Detail, Institute of Illegal Architects.
Stuart Laidlaw and Mike Halliwell.

**FIGURE 3**
Component Detail, Institute of Illegal Architects.
Stuart Laidlaw and Mike Halliwell.

**FIGURE 4**
Exterior, Institute of Illegal Architects.
Edward Woodman.

**FIGURE 5**
Institute of Illegal Architects as Viewed From the RIBA.
Edward Woodman.

**FIGURE 8**
View Along the Length of the Production
Space for Sight Towards the RIBA,
Institute of Illegal Architects.
Edward Woodman.

**FIGURE 9**
View Along the Production Space for Sight
Towards the RIBA, Institute of Illegal Architects.
Edward Woodman.

**FIGURE 10**
View to the North Towards the
Production Spaces for Sight and Sound,
Institute of Illegal Architects.
Edward Woodman.

**FIGURE 11**
The Eye and the Ear,
Institute of Illegal Architects.
Edward Woodman.

**FIGURE 12**
Production Space for Sound,
Institute of Illegal Architects.
Stuart Laidlaw and Mike Halliwell.

**FIGURE 17**
Production Space for Smell,
Institute of Illegal Architects.
Stuart Laidlaw and Mike Halliwell.

**FIGURE 18**
Detail of Cracked Glass Skin,
Production Space for Smell,
Institute of Illegal Architects.
Stuart Laidlaw and Mike Halliwell.

**FIGURE 22**
Production Space for Touch,
Institute of Illegal Architects.
Edward Woodman.

## BIOGRAPHY OF THE AUTHOR

Jonathan Hill is an architect and graduate of the Architectural Association and the Bartlett, University College London. He is a Lecturer at the Bartlett, teaching history, theory and design. His most recent project, THE DEATH OF THE ARCHITECT, was exhibited at the Bartlett in London and Haus der Architektur in Graz, and further developed at Akademie Schloss Solitude in Stuttgart. Hill is the editor of OCCUPYING ARCHITECTURE: BETWEEN THE ARCHITECT AND THE USER.

## ACKNOWLEDGEMENTS

I would like to thank the following individuals for their help with THE ILLEGAL ARCHITECT. I am especially grateful to Bradley Starkey for building the model, which was photographed so well by Edward Woodman, Stuart Laidlaw and Mike Halliwell. For their advice and support I want to thank Xiaochun Ai, Penelope Haralambidou, Lesley Lokko, Frank Lowe, Mark Lumley, Ganit Mayslits, Dr. Philip Tabor, Tan Kay Ngee, Professor Peter Cook and Professor Christine Hawley at The Bartlett, University College London and Roland Ritter at the Haus der Architektur, Graz. I am very grateful to Christian Küsters for the design of the book. Finally, my special thanks go to Duncan McCorquodale of Black Dog Publishing Limited.

## COLOPHON

© 1998 Black Dog Publishing Limited and the author.
Produced by Duncan McCorquodale.
Designed by christian@chkdesign.demon.co.uk.
Printed by Graphite Inc. Limited in the EU.

British Library Cataloguing-in-Publication Data. A catalogue record for this book is available from The British Library. Library of Congress Cataloguing-in-Publication Data: The Illegal Architect

ISBN 1 901033 01 5

Black Dog Publishing Limited
P.O. Box 3082
London NW1 UK
T +44 (0)171 3807500
F +44 (0)171 380 7453